MAKING SOUND

CREATIVE **MUSIC PRODUCTION TIPS**
AND **PHILOSOPHIES**

Table of Contents

Preface

The art of making music has, at least in part, changed a lot over time. Once upon a time it used to be exclusively a communal activity, from early drumming and chanting to orchestras and bands. Nowadays, the creation of music has evolved to become something that is often a solitary activity where one person is self-producing and self-assessing their work. In this sense, the modern music creator sometimes resembles a painter or a sculptor more than a traditional musician.

This book is not a basic course in music production or mixing. It's all about putting new perspectives and creative ideas in your head. The ideas and techniques presented are there to be used right away and ultimately made into your own ideas that find life in your music production work.

A way to approach this book is to read the longer passages in your spare time and keep the tips handy for instant ideas in the studio. You can basically start anywhere and skip ahead as you please. When information in earlier chapters is essential to understanding a concept, I will refer to that chapter or tip.

I've chosen to use the term "music production" in a very broad and modern sense. Today, especially in electronic or sample-based music, music production is pretty much the process from idea to complete arrangement. In this process, mixing is often something that happens along the way. Therefore a lot of the material covered could easily be seen as mix engineering and can be applied to mixing other people's music.

I've tried to be genre-agnostic here, but some tips and techniques will fit some types of music and productions better. It's my hope that you can overcome any prejudice and apply these techniques in an experimental fashion, even though it might not seem to fit your style of music at first glance. The main idea here is to break new creative ground and challenge yourself.

There are a couple of chapters on music theory in this book. The chapters on music theory are written to give a basic and very usable knowledge of the fundamentals of modern western music and the compositional tools that are used today. This is something that is equally important whether you're composing your own music or producing a band or an artist. I find that this sort of information is not easily available to the self-taught music producer of today, so I hope you'll get something useful out of it. I know I have.

The material in this book consists of ideas and philosophies that I've accumulated over the last decade that I've worked professionally with music and audio. Adding to that are my versions of some of the techniques that I've learned from talking to some of the most brilliant people in the industry today, people like Joe Chiccarelli, Tony Maserati and Jack Joseph Puig as well as some other less renowned but nonetheless brilliant engineers.

Each chapter is made up of an introduction to the subject with a few practical ideas followed by a number of self-contained tips relating to that chapter. I hope you find good use for this book.

CREATING DIFFERENT TEXTURES AND MOODS

Music is an extremely powerful sort of stimulus. It's processed – largely unconsciously – by the more primitive parts of our brain, like the amygdala and cerebellum. This is true for aspects like "groove" as well as tonal aspects (major and minor chords, melodic intervals, etc.) and other qualities like tempo and overall texture.

Perhaps more than other art forms, music has the ability to create images and feeling within us that are not necessarily rooted in our memories or prior experiences.

Whether we're talking about songwriting, mixing or production, what we're essentially talking about is the manipulation of mood and texture. These two elements, in turn, set the scene for the emotional response of the listener.

Getting that particular type of response from the listener is always the end goal that should be present in the back of our minds when we're doing any kind of creation, processing or manipulation of sound in our productions.

Is your goal at a certain point in the song a rush of adrenalin or a wash of sentimentality? Do you want the listener to keep listening because the mood is evoking happy feelings or because it resonates with an underlying sense of rebellion?

2. Creating Different Textures and Moods

Don't get me wrong; a lot can be said about the technical skills involved in using a compressor or an EQ, but there really isn't much use in being a technical genius if you don't know what your end goal is. Production and mixing is, in this regard, an extension of songwriting and composition. This is especially true if there are lyrics involved.

The term "prosody" is sometimes used for the matching of lyrical content with the mood of the song or production. A sad phrase may need a minor chord at the end; a happy twist in the lyrics may need the melody to go up, and so on. The effects of mixing and production are maybe not as clear-cut as the effects of songwriting in this regard, but they really do pile up and are essential to a well-executed work of art.

The Foundation

There is research to suggest that the appreciation for music is somewhat dependent on a comprehensible or intuitive structure that generates some sort of predictability as to what will occur next in the song. Interestingly, the song also needs to contain a certain level of the unexpected for the emotional response of the listener to be strong.

As a producer or composer, you can use the listener's expectations to manipulate emotions by choosing when – and when not – to go against those expectations.

So, getting the foundation of a production right is all about making those conscious choices. Choosing the sounds that will add to what you're trying to express, or at least not work against your vision, is a good start. Intuition goes a long way, but intuition can be strengthened a lot by education; namely by studying music similar in style and mood to the music that you want to create. This practice will make it easier for you to know instinctually what will work and what won't.

Pick a track that you find really effective at keeping your interest and that has a good ebb and flow of tension and release. Write out the bars of the track on a piece of paper and note where transitions and fills occur (on what beat of what bar, etc.)

When you look at this map you should be able to see for how many bars the production stays the same and where it changes. You can either write specific things like "shaker comes in" or general things like "two new elements added".

Make a few maps like this. It takes a bit of practice to make ones that have all the relevant information without looking too cluttered, but by the time you've mastered it, you'll a nice little library of road maps for your productions. This is awesome when you get stuck in making loops and not being able to get to a finished arrangement. Also, you'll be more conscious about breaking the rules. (It's usually better that you are aware that you're breaking rules – if not right away, then at least at some later analytical part of your creative process.)

Apart from choosing the sounds and instruments, choosing a tempo is something that is best done in an early stage; if not, things can get pretty messy. Another element, related to tempo, is time signature and groove. Is standard 4/4 time the only way to go? Is the beat based on sixteenth notes, straight eighth notes or triplets?

Working out the best tempo for the song (unless you're working in a genre with pretty much a standard tempo) is often most easily done by playing a stripped down version of the song.

Just playing or humming the melody while finding the tempo with your body, tapping your foot or nodding along is a great way to do it in my experience. While you're at it, why not work out the basic groove too? You will have a lot of the work already done at this point and working out a drum beat and bass line will be much less of a hit-and-miss experience.

5. Creating Different Textures and Moods

EQ

Equalization is one of the most powerful tools in sound design and it's really helpful to educate yourself a bit about the frequency spectrum before boosting or attenuating too aggressively. This involves getting to know your mixing room and where its problem frequencies are, what frequencies are naturally boosted and attenuated.

Let's have a quick look at the Fletcher–Munson curve. What this graph shows is the sensitivity of our hearing at different frequencies and at different amplitudes. The ranges where the lines go upwards are where our ears are less sensitive. The downward dips indicate that we are extra-sensitive at those frequencies.

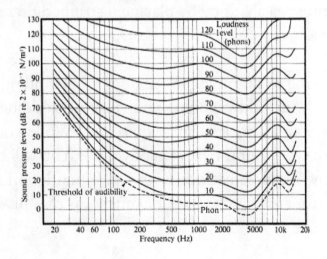

If you look at the low frequencies, from 20 Hz to 100 Hz, you'll see that we are less sensitive to those when we hear them at lower volumes.

At around 80 dBSPL our hearing becomes more linear and more representative of our average hearing than at quieter levels. That's why a lot of advice about mixing states that you should mix at a 80–85 dB level most of the time. This, like most general advice, is best taken with a grain of salt; a lot of professionals mix at a much quieter volume, it's all about learning how a mix should sound at the level at which you are comfortable working.

If you look further up the frequency spectrum you'll see a dip in the curve, a dip that is pretty consistent across all sound pressure levels (SPL). This is the range between approximately 2 kHz and 5 kHz. This is an important frequency range for the human species; this is where you find a baby crying and the intelligibility of speech. No wonder we're so sensitive in this area.

Since we're programmed to pay attention to these frequencies, we can use them to manipulate the listener when we want the her to pay attention to something in our music.

Use this frequency range when you want something to sound more aggressive or upfront (boost), or to mellow something out or make it sound smoother and more "polite" (attenuate).

Using multi-band compression or dynamic EQ to suppress those frequencies when they cross a chosen threshold is a great way to get your mix smoother and more polished. For instance, if you want to draw attention to a delay effect without having it super loud, boost the 2–5 kHz range and they will stand out in the mix. This will allow you turn them down too, and get a bit more room down in the lower mids.

If you want to go further in making something sound smoother and gentler, use a low pass filter on most of the tracks in your mix. Cut at around 12–16 kHz. Leave a few tracks full frequency, perhaps vocals and shakers/hi-hats.

To make something sound grainier and rougher, like the vintage recordings of yesteryear, limit the frequency bandwidth. Check out Tip Number 1 for some ideas on how to perfect a vintage sound using modern recordings.

The low end has a lot of emotional impact on the listener. Introducing the deep bass at a well-chosen moment can be very effective in engaging the listener, and letting the bass in the chorus extend a little bit lower or be a dB or two louder can work really well.

Put a spectrum analyzer on tracks you like the sound of and study what they look like, check out the balance between different parts of the frequency spectrum. Don't follow things like this blindly, but go ahead and make some notes and see if you can get results closer to your ideals by adjusting your own mixes to be more similar to your favorite ones.

Compression

There is a lot you can do with a compressor. Of course, the original idea was to limit the dynamic range of an audio signal, and equalization was about making up for attenuated frequencies, thus making the output more equal to the input. It's safe to say we've found other uses beside the initial ones.

Compression is a very powerful tool for injecting some excitement and movement into a track, but it can just as easily tame the inappropriately hedonistic grooves or make something more intimate.

Let's not get too technical, but we should have a look at what can be achieved with the different parameters that are involved in compression.

Attack can really be used as a sort of EQ that can bring something to the front of attention by brightening the transients. This is done by using a slow attack (let's say 30 milliseconds and more), which will let the first part of the transients be pointy, a quality that is enhanced due to the later part of the transient and sustain being pushed down.

Using a really fast attack (start at around 3 milliseconds) will substantially darken a sound by pushing down the early part of the transients. This can create a more mellow kind of vibe whereas the slower attack will create a more energetic, in-your-face sound. You can achieve a similar effect with a transient designer by adjusting the attack.

The release of a compressor can contribute similar things to the vibe of a track. But here it's the other way around: a fast release will inject energy and movement. It will distort the audio signal, especially if the threshold is way down.

A slow release will not create the same motion; it will keep things in check more and create a smoother, more mellow texture. This is more true if the attack is fast – with a slow attack, a slow release will further exaggerate the initial transient, which can result in a pretty snappy and bright sound.

Be careful when choosing the release time; make sure the movement is doing the general groove of the other tracks a favor and is not working against it. When using a slow release you have to take care that the compressor has time to let go of the signal before the next important transient enters.

Distortion

Distortion is arguably the most used tool in music production and audio mixing. Most of the time we don't even think of it as distortion, but it's there. In its broadest sense, distortion means any alteration of a waveform, but this is not a very practical way to think about it, since that would include any processing like EQ, reverb etc.

Few things can transform a bland and boring sound into fistful of attitude and color as quickly as a healthy dose of distortion. Distortion can really give vocals or a lead instrument a sense of urgency and can give it more emotional impact.

Distortion is an effective form of compression – a well-known fact for anyone who has played an electric guitar through a distortion pedal. Distortion evens out the peaks and you'll end up needing less compression and limiting. A tasteful amount of distortion can make a sound appear more finished or polished.

Mixer Dave Pensado calls distortion "a rich collection of harmonics", and this is a huge part of the benefit of distortion: added harmonics. Harmonics in the upper mid will give your tracks more presence without the need of more EQ (and the risk of added phase issues in your signal) and at the same time give your track a bit more attitude, or "hair" if you will.

This is actually just a different side of the compression effect we just mentioned. Look at a perfect sine wave. It has nice round peaks and no harmonics whatsoever. If you flatten the top of a sine wave you'll get a ... square wave! A square wave has tons of harmonics. Both the compression and the added harmonics are a side effect of clipping, or saturating (essentially the same thing), as we've mentioned.

Transitions

Relating back to what was said about an understandable song structure, transitions are a major piece of the puzzle to help the listener make sense of your music. It is also essential in making sure your chorus has maximum impact.

Working with volume automation is a great way to add some drama to a transition and thereby make the following section more effective. Making just the first two beats of the chorus a little louder can increase the impact of the whole chorus, since our brain doesn't easily notice that the volume goes back to normal. This has to be done within reason, of course, a couple of dB is usually just right. You can also drop a few dB just before the chorus.

The recipe for greater impact is often greater contrast. Let the chorus have longer reverbs, a tad more distortion on the drums, put guitars or synths in stereo instead of mono, etc.

Tip Number 1. Make Anything Sound Vintage

If you want anything to sound more like an old recording, there are a few tricks you can employ. Start by inserting an EQ. Use a low pass filter or low shelving filter to get rid of some of the low end, then do the same with the top end.

Try boosting with a bell curve at around 2 k and insert a tape emulation or any other of your favorite saturation tools. Finish off with a vintage-sounding reverb if you want. A mono plate can really do the trick if it fits the sound you're after.

Tip Number 2. Using Lo-Fi Microphones for Doubling Vocals

A very common production technique is to double the lead vocals in the chorus or sometimes in the verses as well.

If you're using a hi-fidelity condenser mic as your main mic, then doubling that performance with a more low-fi mic like a Shure SM57 can make the performance cut through better in the mix and give it a little more edge in certain parts of the song – most of the time you'll be wanting to use this in the chorus.

In a more sound design-heavy version of this technique you can use really colored mics like the Shure Green Bullet and double the vocal twice and let the takes with the colored mic be panned to the sides and keep the hi-fi mic in the center. This gives the vocals an edgier sound while not abandoning the more polished sound.

Tip Number 3. "Queen" Background Vocal Technique

The band Queen is known for a lot of things, and great background vocals is definitely one of them.

There are a number of ways to record and mix background vocals. Usually, at the root of it, what is being sung is a three-note chord that corresponds to the harmony of the track at that moment in time. One way to record it is to use one singer, usually the lead singer of the group, and record one note of the chord at a time, probably doubling every note three or more times.

While it can sound fine recording one person doing all the notes, there is a hollowness to the sound compared to when a group of people are singing together.

That brings us to the second technique, where each person sings one note of the chord. So now you have three people singing one note each. This definitely gives more color and thickness than the previous technique.

The way Queen did their background vocals was to record one note at a time but to have all of them sing the note together. Then they went on to the next note and all sang that one together and so on. This produces really full and beautiful sounding background vocals that are hard to beat. Of course, it helps to have excellent singers at your disposal.

Tip Number 4. The Magic of Pre-Emphasis and De-Emphasis

Pre-emphasis and de-emphasis were initially used to reduce tape hiss in recordings. The theory was that, by adding a lot of high end before the sound hit tape and then cutting the same amount of high end afterwards, you'd get the same amount of high end but a lot of the high-frequency tape hiss would be attenuated in the process.

Aside from using the technique for its original purpose, there are some interesting sound design applications where it can be put to use:

1. Before your distortion plugin or hardware, use an EQ and boost and sweep until you get the distortion unit to break up and distort in a color that you like. Put an EQ after distortion and cut the frequency previously boosted to balance the frequency spectrum while preserving the color of the distortion. You may have to do some additional EQ in the high end to tame the new harmonics slightly.

2. Do the same thing, but with compression rather than distortion; boost the low end to get the compressor pumping, then attenuate the low end after the compressor.

3. Cut frequencies with a transparent EQ and boost them back up with a colored EQ of your choice.

Tip Number 5. Frequency Split Transient Shaping

Duplicate the kick drum track onto two new ones so that you'll have three kick drum tracks in total. Let the first track only keep the frequencies up to 80 Hz, bandpass filter the second one to contain only the frequencies between 80 Hz and 1500, and leave the third track with only frequencies above 1500 Hz.

Put a transient designer on the first two tracks. Now you can turn up the attack on the bandpass-filtered track do make the kick drum really knock; and turn up the sustain on the first track to get a longer sub tone that rings out. Adjust until it has the best of both worlds. Listen to the original kick without processing and compare to your new layered sound to make sure you're not losing anything important in the process.

Try this also on a synth bass or even bass guitar.

Tip Number 6. New York Compression

This is a famous parallel compression technique that is used on drums. The technique was used extensively by New York engineers in the 1990s, but a similar technique was also used earlier by Motown engineers.

On the drum bus, send a bit of the signal to an aux and set up a compressor and an EQ on the aux track. The compression should be quite aggressive, a ratio of at least 10:1 is preferable, attack time around 3 ms as a starting point. The release time can be fast for more aggressive, pumping, compression or slower if the track needs a mellower sound. About 10 dB of gain reduction is needed for you to get the most out of this technique.

Boost 1–3 dB at 100 Hz and 10 kHz to add to the weight and crack of the drums.

Lastly, send a bit of the bass track to the aux to glue the whole rhythm section and adjust the send on the drum bus until you have enough of the effect in the mix.

Tip Number 7. Parallel Processing

Parallel processing is an amazing technique that could really open up a world of mixing and sound design tools. The idea and huge benefit of all parallel processing is that you keep the original signal untouched while blending in the processed signal to your liking.

This is great because while heavy compression or distortion might sound really awesome, certain things can get lost in the process (transients might lose definition, the low end might lose some of its fullness, etc.) that can be very hard to get back.

Mix engineers like Andrew Scheps and Tony Maserati are using this technique extensively for these very reasons. See the New York compression tip for ideas on parallel compression.

Distortion can be used in parallel to great effect. Either you distort the whole frequency spectrum and blend it in to change the overall character of the sound, or you use parallel distortion as an exciter. What this means is that you choose a part of the frequency spectrum that you want to give more presence, or excite, by boosting the harmonics through distortion. For example, on the parallel channel, use an EQ to filter out everything except the high end. Or distort just the low mids and blend it in for some extra weight.

As an alternative to plain distortion, using guitar amp/cabinet emulations in parallel is a great way to make something cut through a mix or to make a virtual instrument sound a little more real.

Then, of course, effects like phaser and chorus work great used subtly in parallel; using a little bit of phaser on a loop can make it seem more organic and give it some variation.

Tip Number 8. Match EQ Tricks

A match EQ lets you analyze the frequency spectrums of two different sounds, then it calculates the difference and applies an EQ curve on the chosen target tracks so that it approximates the first track's frequency balance.

One use for this can be to compare your mix to a reference track and get a general idea about EQ choices you can make to make it sound closer to your reference track.

There are more creative applications for this type of tool, though. One of my favorites is to use an old vinyl record or a sample of one as the source track. It can be a drum break, a vocal or a full mix.

Once you've analyzed the sound clip you can apply it to something in your production, like drums, piano, vocals, synths, pretty much anything and it will have a retro sound that can be hard to achieve by just EQing manually.

One word of advice, however: there is a slider on most, if not all, match EQs; turn it down a lot. Letting it operate at 100% gives you a result that is usually unusable. Around 20% is a good starting point. There is also usually a knob that lets you smooth out the curve a bit, also a good idea for more natural-sounding results.

Tip Number 9. Two Master Bus EQ Tricks

Using an EQ on the master is something most mixers do. Here are two ways to use it to your advantage:

1. Start your mix by inserting an EQ with a high shelving curve at around 10 or 12 kHz. Boost a few dB since you'll end up brightening most of your tracks, why not take care of it on the master bus and do less processing on individual tracks? You save time and possibly end up with less phase distortion adding up.

2. Sweep the master bus EQ to find the frequencies that make the mix sound harsh or muddy; instead of trying to correct it on the master, go through the individual tracks and see which ones have a lot of energy at those frequencies, cut a dB or so on each track. (If you have lots of tracks, cutting something like 0.2 dB on several might cure the problem in a very transparent way.)

Tip Number 10. EQ into Compression

This is a trick that is used by a lot of mixers, especially on lead vocals, where you need lots of presence for them to cut through a dense mix, but you don't want the vocals to be ear-piercingly harsh.

First insert an EQ, followed by a compressor. Then boost the high mids or treble frequencies for presence and bite. What happens is that when you boost these frequencies before the compressor, you change the frequencies that go into the side-chain of the compressor and therefore change the behavior of the compression.

What this means in plain English is that you make the compressor more sensitive to the frequencies that you boost, making it clamp down on those frequencies. You'll end up with a frequency spectrum that is changed overall but with a time-based effect that controls the peaks and kills those over-the-top, harsh sounds.

You can get more radical with compression and achieve more presence with less harshness.

Tip Number 11. A Few Essential Frequencies

Cut the "mud" frequencies to let the lower bass frequencies shine and provide a solid bottom for your track. The legendary engineer Ken Scott (The Beatles, Pink Floyd, David Bowie, etc.) is known for cutting around 200 Hz to get a better bass sound.

To get a thick and heavy sounding snare, boosting around 100 Hz will really make it hit your chest. It's always best to start out with a sample that is close to what you want, of course.

Two frequencies you can use in mastering or during mixing to get a bit more transient energy happening are 80Hz and 5 kHz. They pretty much correspond to the energy in the kick drum and snare drum.

Tip Number 12. MIDI Sends

MIDI can be used effectively to bring a simple arrangement to life without changing the actual notes. First, program all the MIDI on the number of MIDI tracks needed. Then set up a number of synths (hardware or software), string libraries, etc, and choose the MIDI track(s) as input on all the instruments and instrument tracks.

You now have a number of instruments receiving the same note values. Now the fun starts. Use volume automation to make an arrangement. Start with the faders completely down on all except one or two tracks, then ride the faders to make different combinations of instruments in different sections of the song.

Play around with contrasts like sparse versus dense arrangement and automate filters and other parameters for more variety and organic feel.

Tip Number 13. Reverb Mute Trick

Surprise effects can be very effective in a song, even when they are quite subtle.

Using a longish reverb on a vocal and then suddenly cutting it out for a phrase is a cool sounding effect that is heard on the Tory Amos song A Kinda Fairytale and Elvis Costello's Beyond Belief.

Try using this technique on instruments as well. Put some reverb on the drums and mute the reverb during a fill, or try other types of effects and surprise the listener with a couple of beats of dry sound.

Another way to go about it is to do the opposite, but use other effects like delay on a track and let a phrase or two ring out into a long reverb.

Tip Number 14. Reverb Exciter Trick

This is a very interesting trick. It can sound subtle or it can give you a bit of a surreal feel. It's mainly used to give a bit of excitement to a vocal or lead instrument.

Start by duplicating the track you want to give this treatment. Pitch shift the duplicated track up one octave. Change the send to pre fader and send the pitch-shifted track to a reverb. Turn down the fader of the dry channel so that all you can hear is the reverb.

Use the high pitch reverb as the only reverb for the original lead track or blend it with a reverb that's fed by the non-pitch shifted signal. This technique will excite the top end and give your sound more presence in a mix.

Tip Number 15. Transient Designer Guitar Trick

Guitar recordings featuring arpeggios or any type of single string playing can benefit a lot from transient designers.

Turning up the attack can make the performance sound a lot more confident and played with more intention.

Turning down the sustain a little bit can also help you deal with unwanted string noise or leakage from headphones or other instruments in the room.

NATURALISM

Sometimes you're producing or mixing music that consists of instruments played live by musicians in a natural space. Or you're trying to create the illusion of such a context. In those cases the mindset is very different from the mindset that you need when creating music (electronic or otherwise) that has no point of reference in the natural world.

When producing music that doesn't need to sound like something created in a real room, using instruments with resonating parts like strings or drumheads, you can really go to extremes in sound design – at least as long as what you're creating is acceptable in the genre (if any) in which you're operating.

To Record or Not to Record

Today it's easier than ever to make a recording. You need a minimal amount of equipment and it can be done practically anywhere. Still, getting the sound you're after is not always the easiest thing in the world.

There are so many things that need to be up to standard for a recording to be stellar: a decent instrument played by a good player in a room that is as dead or live as needed and has a good tone, a microphone that's up for the job, and a signal chain with enough quality to capture the good parts without introducing too much hiss and unwanted distortion.

Even if you have all these things in order you still need to know how to capture the performance well, whether it's about the choice of microphone, where to place it, how to angle it, or how to make the player perform at his very best and make the right choices for the song in question. These are the roles of the audio engineer and the producer, and this work is done in real time and can be very challenging, especially if you hire a session player and have limited time to pull it off.

In my opinion, there are few better ways to make your track more interesting than recording your own sounds. However, it's wise to know your limitations. Layering and combining samples, virtual instruments and your own recordings is a great way to go.
Record things you are able to do well enough to not change your vision of the production too much. Use samples, loops and virtual instruments for the rest, and keep practicing your recording skills and try to get to know more musicians along the way.

The term "convincing" is something that comes up a lot in my head when I try to make something somewhat artificial sound natural and real. There are an abundance of techniques that can be used in order to make something sound more like the real thing. Two things often used in productions are loops and virtual instruments. Let's have a look at those two.

Making Loops More Realistic

Loops, especially rhythmic loops, are a kind of basic building block for a lot of productions. In what I call naturalistic productions, shaker loops and percussion loops are perhaps the most common types of loops.

There are several ways to make loops sound more realistic and "human" (check out Tip Number 20 for one of my personal favorites). If possible, use long loops that don't repeat as often. If you're using a four-bar loop or an eight-bar loop, cut it up so that it repeats every three bars or every seven bars (this works better for percussion loops where there's no kick drum). By doing this you'll have accents, fills and other rhythmic little patterns happening in different places in the arrangement. This goes a long way to make it sound less like a static loop.

Automation is probably the most powerful tool at your disposal when it comes to making something sound more like a real instrument played by a musician. If you have something like a hi-hat loop or a percussion loop, start by doing some volume automation. Make small moves, a few dB up or down here and there.

Next step is to insert an EQ and activate a mid-range band – use a bell curve with a medium-wide Q value. Automate the gain on the EQ band so that it boosts slightly and comes down to zero and then attenuates slightly and so on. You can also automate the frequency center for some extra realism. Make small moves and be careful not to make it sound like a synthesizer filter effect.

Making Virtual Instruments Work

Virtual instruments are fantastic tools that can let you realize the sounds you hear in your head without the need for a band or an expensive string quartet or orchestra. They are very affordable in comparison with the real thing and you can find versions of most real instruments that you can imagine.

There is a catch, however; they can sound rather lifeless and it can take a bit of effort to make them sound close to the real thing, since a virtual instrument usually is capable of things that the original is not.

One very important thing that a lot of people seem to forget is research. Unless you know how to play the instrument you are emulating, chances are that you need a bit of education regarding the physics of the instrument and how it is usually played by a professional player.

I would suggest doing a bit of reading about the instruments, especially if you're working with orchestral instruments that you're not super-familiar with. After that bit of theoretical research, it's time to listen and listen some more to recordings of that instrument. Don't start programming your MIDI parts before you have a really good idea of how it should sound when it's done.

If you're programming brass or woodwinds, it's a good idea to sing the parts to make sure the phrases are not so long that they would be impossible to play without taking a breath.

I'm not saying that you can't improvise and experiment with the parts; I'm saying that the tone and the feel and the mechanics of the instruments should be close to second nature before you're ready to program a convincing part.

Drums

When programming a virtual drum kit it is essential that the drum beat in question is physically possible. There are a huge number of examples of virtual drummers that would've needed three or four arms to pull off the drum beat in question.

The next thing to look out for is that the dynamics and choices of rhythms fit the music. Again, if you're not a drummer yourself, you should listen extensively to drummers playing similar music to what you're producing.

When the programming is up to par, it's time to look at some processing that can help you get a more realistic sound. A problem with a lot of virtual instruments is that they sound too clean and neutral, which might make them versatile but doesn't really make them sound "like a record".

If you have any outboard gear, especially the more colored kind, now might be the time to use it. Processing a virtual drum track through a real tape machine can really transform it to something really usable. It doesn't have to be super expensive either, check out the chapter Great Analog Gear on the Cheap for some ideas.

Any kind of distortion used lightly can round out the edges and make the instrument more authentic-sounding.

To get some real-world analog processing, mic up your monitor speakers. You can either close-mic them with a colorful microphone or put them in a good-sounding room (some people swear by using a bathroom for this) and move the microphones around the room until it sounds good. You now have a reverb that you can record to a new track and blend in for some realism.

As an alternative, you can use a good convolution reverb, although keep in mind that it will be a more static sound since it doesn't respond to different frequencies and amplitude.

Strings

Another common example we're going to have a look at is string libraries. There are a lot of things to consider when you're programming string parts in a song. First, as mentioned earlier, educate yourself on the basics of the instruments: the ranges, different articulations, dynamics, etc.

What might be even more important when it comes to string programming is knowing a little bit about string arrangement. For instance, if you play chords like you might do on a piano, with the notes close together, chances are that your strings will sound more like an accordion.

One of the things that makes a real orchestra sound so full and rich is the slight difference in tone and timing that happens between the individual players. There are some ways to approximate this.

Using more than one string library is a common and generally good practice for a couple of reasons. First, almost every string library has its strengths and weaknesses; some articulations sound good and others not so much.

The other reason is to get a more realistic sound by layering parts. You get the benefit of the differences in tone and timing that I mentioned, and hopefully it will cover up some of the weaknesses in the scripting and the samples themselves, as well as your programming.

Another way which may or may not be possible for you is to layer the string arrangement with a real player. Getting a violin player to double the violin parts a couple of times and blend that recording with the MIDI parts can really increase the realism a lot.

If you don't have more than one string library and no affordable string players are within reach, there is still a technique you can employ that will give you a bit of that realistic blend of timbres. What you do is you pitch shift the samples up a few semitones and transpose the MIDI down by the same number of semitones. With a second double, you do the opposite. This way the samples will be in tune with each other but will have slightly different timbre because they will not be the same recorded notes.

Just as with drums, I would suggest experimenting with tape saturation and other light distortion to smooth out the edges of the sometimes unnaturally clean sounds. And for all types of sample-based instruments, adding some noise like tape hiss can fill in the gaps and make it sound more believable.

34. Naturalism

Tip Number 16. Doubling Tricks

When you're recording a lead part and think about doubling it, there is a good rule of thumb in classical arranging theory. The rule goes like this: when arranging lead melodies, either have one instrument or three instruments play the line in unison (same notes, same octave), not two.

The reason for this is that the timbre and difference in intonation will sound more balanced this way. So, try having three guitars or synthesizers play a line next time. See if you like it better than two.

Using a tool like Melodyne, you can create a very polished sound by having a more natural-sounding vocal take panned center while you have an extremely tuned version panned left or right. You can also flatten the vibrato – it will sound very unnatural on its own but will sound good blended with the unprocessed version.

To make a version that can be panned to the opposite side (remember: three parts is a good idea when doubling), either tune the notes a little bit less than the first double, or mess with the formants to give it a slightly different timbre.

A very subtle doubling trick you can try is to record a second take and feed that only to the reverb, muting the dry sound sent to the reverb completely.

Tip Number 17. The Earplug Recording Trick

When recording an instruments or group of instruments in a room, there are a few things to consider. Putting aside monumentally important things like finding the right player and the right instrument for the job (let's assume you're stuck with what you've got for now), microphone position is arguably the most important thing.

Even though you'll hear a lot of opinions on the importance of choosing the right microphone, the right preamplifier, or the right EQ for the job, nothing will change the sound more than moving the microphone to another position.

A great way to find the right placement is to put an earplug into one ear and walk around in the room or move your head near the instrument you're recording. Using only one ear you'll be able to get closer to what a mono microphone is hearing. Find the sweet spot (the place where it sounds the most like what you'd want it to sound coming out of your monitors) and place the microphone there. Take the angle into consideration too when doing this.

Be careful not to damage your hearing when doing this, make sure the sound is not too loud.

Tip Number 18. Re-amp the Snare Drum

A really neat trick when you're using any kind of drum samples is to use a small speaker and place it face down on top of a real snare drum.

Put a microphone under the snare and play back the sample snare drum beat through the speaker and record the real snare.

Now you need to line up the tracks in your DAW (Digital Audio Workstation), then nudge the recorded track until you get the best sound possible with the combined tracks.

Tip Number 19. Using a Real Room to Enhance Other Reverbs

I got this tip when interviewing producer and engineer Joe Chiccarelli in 2015. He likes to use real physical spaces when they're available. And there's a theory to go with the practice.

Using one single real space in your mix can make a difference in how we perceive the other digital reverbs. It can fool the ear into interpreting the rest of the reverbs in the mix as being real spaces too.

The thing is that the real physical space doesn't have to be the most prominent reverb in the mix, it can be used on some instruments only or on certain vocal tracks. This might sound weird, but recording a real space can make a real difference.

How to go about it: Put one of your monitor speakers (or two for stereo) in a nicely reverberant space in close vicinity. Place the microphone(s) in another part of the room. Bathrooms tend to work well, as do stairwells for longer reverb tails. But your living room might sound great too, especially after some moving of monitors and/or microphones.

Play back the tracks you want to process with your reverb and record the sound reverberating in the room onto a new track in your DAW. Adjust the level of the reverb track instead of the reverb send in your DAW like you normally would.

Tip Number 20. Humanize Your Shaker Loops

Looped shaker parts are very common in modern music production but can easily sound static and lifeless. Volume automation that follows the dynamics of the song is one way to make the shaker parts sound more human and to make them sit better in the mix.

But a real shaker performance doesn't only vary in volume; a softly played shaker will have less transient and more sustain than a loudly played one. A way to address this is to use a transient designer type tool, like SPL's Transient Designer or Logic's Enveloper.

By automating the attack on these plugins you can shape the transient of the shaker in real time. You might find that you can skip most of your volume automation and still end up with an even more natural and "humanized" result. Try this on other types of percussion as well!

If you don't own a tool that lets you shape the transients directly, you can try putting a compressor on the shaker track and automate the attack time (faster attack equals backing off the attack on the transient designer). Parallel compression might be the way to go here to avoid too much change in volume and to get a more subtle, natural result.

Lastly, add a bit more variation by inserting a phaser or flanger on the shaker track, then roll back the dry/wet knob until it's barely noticeable but is missed when you turn it off.

Tip Number 21. Process in Stages

Sometimes we're tempted to do heavy processing with one single compressor or distortion effect, etc. While this might sound great for more extreme and obvious effects, doing it in stages is a great way to transform a sound in more sophisticated ways.

In the old days, there was so much distortion and compression happening naturally through the way things were recorded. There were lots of tubes and transformers in the typical microphones, preamplifiers and mixing consoles used, and everything was recorded to tape, often multiple times. This process sometimes created a very distorted result that nonetheless sounds musical and pleasing to us.

Try putting small amounts of distortion several times on a sound (inserted on the track, on the bus/group of that track, then on the master; or simply several inserts on a track that do very little), or using three compressors with different characteristics that each compress just a couple of decibels.

Remember that distortion/saturation is also compression, meaning that it limits the peaks and makes the signal less dynamic. You can use tape emulations, compressors and distortion boxes to achieve the same thing. Let them all contribute a little bit to the end goal.

Tip Number 22. Do Your Arrangements Elsewhere

Don't do every part of your process like writing, production and mixing in the same place, using the same monitoring, etc.

There is great value in dividing your work and finding the circumstances that work the best for each process. I find that writing, creating new sounds and doing the final mix is best done in my studio using the big monitors that allow me to hear a lot details and at the same time lets me fill the room with sound in those moments when I need a boost of inspiration.

However, when it comes to arrangement, I really prefer sitting with a laptop listening through not so great headphones or through my crappy kitchen radio. In this environment, those cool sounds and mixing tricks that gave me the chills coming through the big monitors don't seem to do much for me.

This is great because it means they won't distract me from focusing on the arrangement of the song. When my focus isn't sonics, I suddenly hear things like kick drum patterns being too busy in the first verse, or that the transition going into the second chorus is really weak.

Generally, when listening on smaller speakers I find that the arrangement is too crowded, and the impact of all the elements coming in at different times becomes clearer to me.

It's great to walk around doing other things and write down notes on a piece of paper whenever you react to something. Then bring the notes to your studio and change things around when listening to your big studio monitors, to make sure that the changes don't hurt the arrangement or mix.

DOWN THE
RABBIT HOLE

ADVANCED
SOUND DESIGN

G etting deep into sound design can be very fun and exciting, but if you're just randomly bending sound you can get lost quite easily and forget what you where looking for in the first place. This can be OK if you're just looking for inspiration and you're creating something from scratch without a clear idea of the end result.

If you're in the middle of a production, however, you'll need some sort of direction in your search for the perfect sound.

Moving Things Around

A great exercise in basic sound design that will improve your understanding of all sorts of audio processing makes use of the standard plugin workflow in your DAW. Start by inserting a chain of plugins on a few prominent tracks in your session. The plugins can be the usual suspects like EQ, a compressor or two, saturation, reverb (use it as an insert using the dry/wet knob for this exercise), delay, chorus, etc.

Put the plugins in the order that you would normally do, and now start moving them around one by one. Listen to how the sound changes when you put the saturation plugin after the reverb instead of before it. How does it affect the sound when you insert the EQ before or after compression or distortion?

Pitch Shifting

Pitch shifting is one of the most powerful sound design tools producers have at their disposal. Every time I get really deep into sound design, pitch shifting is almost always a part of the work. Finding a good workflow in your DAW to quickly try out shifting the pitch of an audio clip, and being able to automate gradual pitch shift, is essential.

Recording high-pitched sounds like metal against glass, the sound of a bunch of keys or certain percussion instruments and then pitching them down by as much as an octave or even more, is a really cool and easy way to create unique sounds. Pitch shifting is almost always the first thing I try when a sound is not exciting or interesting enough. Smaller pitch changes can make a sound (even atonal sounds) fit the track better without changing the character of the sound too much.

Transforming Acoustic Sounds

Next to pitch shifting, applying heavy distortion to a sound is perhaps the simplest way to change it into something completely different and create synth-like textures from acoustic sources. Use a low pass filter to cut out the higher harmonics to get rid of the buzzy part of the sound. Create some stereo movement and change the texture further by applying effects like chorus or phasers.

Creating Glitchy Sounds with Gates

Gates are versatile tools that can be used creatively to great effect. They can be used to transform a drum break or percussion loop into a glitchy loop that really screams for attention.

Start by finding a loop that has the right groove for your track. Insert a gate and bring up the threshold until only the short bursts of transients are heard. Then turn down the release and hold parameters, and play around with the attack time until you get a nice glitchy groove.

Now there are two options: either start processing with compression, distortion, radical EQ, phasing, delay, reverb, etc. or insert a trigger plugin that lets you replace the transients of your loop with samples of your choice. The possibilities are pretty much endless.

Tip Number 23. Reverb Tape-Stop Effect

Tape-stop effects are very common these days and can be very effective. This is a new take on this classic effect and serves the same purpose in an arrangement but in something of a new way.

Record the reverb tail of an instrument or the whole mix at the end of a phrase onto a new track. Automate a good-sounding pitch shift algorithm so that it slowly or abruptly drops in pitch as it decays.

You can either use bigger increments like semitones or drop the pitch in cents for a subtler effect.

Tip Number 24. Kick Drum Rubber Synth Bass

You can make a cool rubbery sounding synth lead or bass sound by using a sampler and a kick drum sample. I've had great results with a sample of an acoustic kick drum played kind of loosely – a bit dull and papery sounding. Load the sample into a sampler and loop the sample so that it starts again every time it has reached the end.

Adjust the start and end of the sample until you have a nice sounding tone that is the same pitch as the key you're pressing; you can change the root key in the sampler to make it appear on the right key, but you need to fine-tune it by ear, or using a tuner.

Distort it slightly (or aggressively if you wish) and boost pretty generously at 1 kHz and apply other effects; phasers work really well to give it depth and make it more interesting. Finally, shape the sound with EQ to make the bass punch and the high end as smooth or aggressive as you want it.

Tip Number 25. Spectral Madness

Tools that are created for different kinds of noise reduction can often be used creatively for sound design. Izotope RX's spectral tool is designed to eliminate a specific part of an audio file – the sound of a door slamming in the middle of a perfect vocal take, for instance.

This is made possible because you're watching a spectrogram which allows you to see what's going on in all frequency ranges over time. You can highlight specific parts of the sound and attenuate it or eliminate it completely.

Such a tool is very effective in making something unwanted disappear while giving you a natural sounding result. However, we're dealing in creative sound design here, so forget about natural for a second; cutting frequency holes in any kind of sound is a really fun way to get extreme and unique results.

This type of workflow cannot really be recreated with EQ automation, and it's really worth a try. Try it on synth sounds or any kind of loops.

Tip Number 26. Two Gating Tricks

Gated reverbs are mostly associated with music from the 1980s where the snare would be sent to a big reverb that abruptly was cut off by a noise gate, causing a majestic and very unnatural effect.

Although this is still a valid technique, there are other uses of gated reverbs that are worth a closer look.

1. Set up a synth and put a reverb followed by a gate on an aux. Use the synth as the input for the gate's side-chain. This way the gate will "see" the synth and will open every time there's a sound coming from the synth, and the gate will close when the sound stops.

Use fast settings on the attack/hold controls so you only hear the reverb while the note is being played. Use a fast setting on the release as well but back it off slightly if you hear a popping sound when the reverb tail is being cut off. Send some of the synth to the aux, dial in a nice big reverb sound (set the pre-delay to 0 so the reverb comes in as soon as the note is played), and start playing the synth.

The reverb will be heard whenever the synth plays, and will be cut off the moment the synth's sound is lower than the gate's threshold. This way you'll get no reverb tails muddying up the mix and can use a bigger reverb sound than you otherwise could. This is a great way to get a huge synth lead or pad while making room for the other instruments.

2. This time, change the gate to a compressor. As before, use the synth as the side-chain input. Now when playing the synth the reverb gets attenuated by the compressor and lets the synth through dry and unaffected. When the synth stops playing, the reverb comes in. If you set the compressor's release time right, the reverb will produce a nice swelling sound that can be very striking.

Tip Number 27. The Chinese Rattle-Drum MIDI Trick

Chinese rattle-drums are hand-held drums with two heads facing outward that are struck by pellets connected to the drum by a cord. The drum is mounted on a rod that is twisted back and forth with the player's hands; this causes the pellets to strike the drumheads in a rhythmic but slightly haphazard fashion.

Rhythms like these that are regular in nature but very much alive and organic are cool to record and convert to MIDI notes. This conversion can be done with tools like Melodyne or inside some DAWs.

The rhythmic information can be used for percussive fills or even synth arpeggio parts. Just move the notes vertically to the right notes. If you don't have a rattle-drum at hand, recording a rubber ball bouncing on the table top is a good alternative. Since the drum roll (or bouncing ball) slows down naturally until it stops, it can work really well to slow down a track and take it into a big ambient break.

Tip Number 28. Swelling Distortion Reverb

Reverbs are sometimes overlooked when it comes to sound design. There are, however, a lot of fun things you can do with reverbs. This one is a little more on the unusual side and can work great as a subtle fill at the end of a four-bar section.

You can do this processing directly on the aux where your reverb is inserted, but to have greater control it might be wise to record the reverb onto an audio track.

Insert a distortion unit after the reverb or as a first insert if you've recorded the reverb to an audio track. After the distortion, insert a compressor. Automate the gain on the distortion unit or use a gain plugin before the distortion unit to drive it hot.

Let the compressor even out the increase in gain, so that you'll get an increasingly distorted signal while keeping the amplitude roughly the same. A bit of volume automation (attenuation) after the compressor may be needed since the increased harmonic content will make the signal appear louder, which may or may not be what you want.

Experiment with how fast and how much you can increase the distortion; it usually works really well as a fill for half a bar.

Tip Number 29. Design a Synth Snare Drum

Here's a quick way to make a classic drum machine-type snare drum using a standard subtractive synthesizer.

1. Turn up a simple sine wave oscillator and open up the cut-off filter.

2. Turn up the white noise generator.

3. Play a low note on the keyboard (not sub-bass territory, slightly above that) and start adjusting the amp ADSR curve. Start by turning down the attack, turning up the decay slightly, no sustain and optionally a bit of release. This should give you a snappy sound that is a good starting point.

4. Play around with the cut-off and resonance to fine-tune the sound.

5. Insert a compressor and compress the snare with a slowish attack and medium release to enhance the punch of the sound.

6. Complete the sound design by experimenting a bit with distortion/saturation, reverb and delay.

Tip Number 30. Use IR Reverb to Make a Ghostly Vocal Effect

This is a great way to sort of preview a hook early on in a tune in an eerie, almost subliminal way. Load up your vocal hook as a sample into a convolution reverb.

Make a rhythmic pattern to trigger the reverb, and you'll get a weird-sounding version of the original sample that makes for a great intro to a song or transition to a verse or chorus.

As always, experiment. It can be used on other sources than vocals. Let me know what you come up with.

Tip Number 31. Tempo-Synced Reverb Tremolo

There's a lot of fun things you can do to your reverb sends. Apart from filters, tremolos might be the next brilliant thing to reach for. It will give you some movement in the stereo field when done in stereo and you'll an overall wider sensation of a wider mix, or it can just move and groove to the rhythm of the track in mono.

In stereo, try using different rhythmic values for the left channel and the right channel, like eighth-notes on one side and sixteenth-notes on the other. Triplets can also be very cool in this context; you can use different rhythms for different parts of the song or just use the tremolo briefly in a section as a nice effect. In the latter context you can use it less subtly since you really want the effect to be noticed.

You even use one tremolo going into another one, where one is slower and the other one is faster; let one be mixed in more subtly than the other one.

Tip Number 32. Strange Snare Reverb

Make a synth pad track that follows the chords of the track. Insert a reverb on that track and make sure it's 100% wet so no dry signal comes through. Next, insert a gate after the reverb. Using the side-chain of the gate, let the snare trigger the gate so that it opens every time the snare hits.

Adjust the release on the gate until it sounds good. You now have some ambiance around each snare hit or a snare reverb tail with no snare in it, depending on the release time of your gate. Experiment with other types of sounds to replace the synth pad: try a shaker or an acoustic guitar.

Also try sending the reverb signal into a second reverb to smooth out the gate's release. Put an EQ last and shape the sound until it fits in the mix.

Tip Number 33. Rhythmic Loop Phase Trick

When using various rhythmic loops in your arrangement, interesting sounds can be created by carefully messing with the micro timing of your tracks.

Try moving one of the tracks back or forward in samples or milliseconds. Try one before the other and see which one yields the most interesting result.

Often tonal sounds can appear and the sum is very different from its parts. This is one of those things that usually just happens by chance, but since the result can be extremely rewarding, it is certainly worth trying as a conscious technique.

FINISH YOUR PRODUCTIONS AND GET MORE DONE

Most of us enjoy experimenting and playing around with sounds and musical ideas, but actually finishing your work can sometimes be the hardest thing. Having a plan is a good idea. Here I present a number of tools that you can test for yourself and decide what works well for you.

Temptation Bundling

If you struggle to get started working on your music productions or you find yourself skipping the hard parts of the process too often, temptation bundling might be the cure for you. It's a pretty simple technique that uses your temptations to force you to do the things that tend to create a bit of resistance in you, or things that you simply forget to do.

This technique has proven effective in studies regarding exercise habits and is well worth a try.

Start by creating a list with two columns next to each other. In the first column, write down a number of things that are pleasurable to you, tempting activities that you find yourself doing instead of working on your music.

In the second column, write down the tasks that you would like to perform more often but tend to procrastinate over.

Now take a look at the two lists and see if you can link something from the left column with something on the right. The idea is that you're only allowed to do the tempting activity after you've performed the task in the second column to which you've linked it.

The Eisenhower Box

Dwight Eisenhower was the 34th president of the United States and was a man known to be extremely productive over very long periods of time.

He had a simple strategy that is used to organize tasks into different categories, which will help you plan your work days and weeks. These tasks can be either professional or personal, it doesn't really matter.

There are four categories:

1. Urgent and important.
2. Important but not urgent.
3. Urgent but not important.
4. Neither urgent nor important.

Let's take a look at each one of the categories. The first one should contain tasks that are important in the sense that they contribute to our long-term goals or will have severe consequences if they're not dealt with. They should also be urgent; if they're not done soon, you'll have negative consequences. It is quite easy to see that tasks that fill those conditions need to be performed right away. They also usually need to be performed by you personally. Examples of this category are deadlines, crises, and problems that need to be solved quickly.

The second category is for tasks that are important, that are contributing to our long-term goals or will have severe negative consequences if not done. In this case, though, time is not really such an issue. They can be done later. These tasks can involve working on relationships or planning for future events.

The third category contains tasks that are urgent in the sense that they need to be dealt with quickly but they are not important to your long-term goals. These kinds of things should be delegated to someone else or rescheduled if possible. These kinds of tasks can either be interruptions by other people (asking for meetings or your opinion/decision), or they can be related to things like answering emails or making a phone call to schedule something.

The last category is for things that are neither important nor urgent. These are things like watching your favorite TV show, or checking social media. It can also be things that someone else wants you to do. Eliminate those as much as possible.

	Urgent	Not Urgent
Important	DO IT NOW	PLAN IT Schedule a time to do it
Not Important	DELEGATE IT Who can do it for you?	DROP IT Eliminate it

Timers

Timers are really powerful tools. They are great for getting things done by limiting the time you're working on a specific task. Timers can also make you aware of how much time you need for each task.

Doing something that you're reluctant to do, like replying to an anxiety-inducing email, is a lot easier if you have a timer set for 10 minutes in front of you. Knowing that there's only this short, limited time that you need to deal with this task makes it a lot easier to start it. Even when the task itself is likely to take more than 10 minutes, committing yourself to doing 10 minutes of work will oftentimes get you started enough that you'll end up finishing the whole task. And if you only do the 10 minutes, at least you've started!

The Pomodoro technique is a great technique based on the use of timers ("pomodoro" means "tomato" in Italian and refers to the tomato-shaped kitchen timers). The basis of the Pomodoro technique is using a timer and setting it for 25 minutes. This 25 minutes equals one pomodoro. During this pomodoro you're not allowed to let any distractions like checking your email get in your way.

When using this technique you'll keep track of how many pomodoros a specific task will take you to do. This will give you more control and predictability when planning your work and you will get to know your own capacity better.

Timers that have a very clear visual representation of time are especially suited for these kinds of technique

CBT

Cognitive behavioral therapy is a form of therapy that mainly targets our behaviors and thinking patterns. There are a number of tools in CBT for analyzing our behaviors, some of which could be of help when it comes to improving our effectiveness as music producers.

Are you spending a lot of time making loops, going through synth presets, listening to your unfinished productions on high volume, nodding your head to the music? Are you spending a lot less time mapping out arrangements, working on transitions and finishing your mixes? The first category would be what we'll call behavioral excess; the latter is called behavioral deficit.

Make a list of behavioral excesses (things of which you to do much), and behavioral deficits (things of which you do too little). Now you should have a pretty good view of your situation; the task now is to start increasing the amount of time you perform the tasks in the behavioral deficit list, and to decrease the amount of time you spend on the things in the behavioral excess list. Use this as a basis for writing out a work schedule for yourself.

You can combine this with the temptation bundling technique. Use your behavioral deficit list as your second column and pair the items up with things or activities that you desire.

Reminders and Deadlines

Sometimes, even with the best of intentions, we get distracted and fail to do some important task. Distractions nowadays are ubiquitous, so having a system to keep you on track seems wise.

Having an alarm on your phone with a reminder of some key things from your to-do list of the day can work well. Writing things down and having automated reminders will free up your mind from the burden of having to remember everything. This practice by itself can increase your creativity. This is a key aspect of the notorious Getting Things Done approach.

Deadlines are a necessity for most of us. Without them we tend to float aimlessly and get stuck not making choices, getting too deep into details and the pursuit of perfection. If you're not involved in a project where other people expect you to finish something at a particular time, you need to create your own deadlines.

It is important, to make a deadline effective, that there is some sort of consequence if the deadline is not met. The most obvious way to do this is to include other people in some way, so that you're held accountable if you fail to achieve what you set out to achieve. The motivation is usually to avoid losing face, but go ahead and be creative when creating consequences for yourself.

THE
POWER
OF
CONTRAST

One of the main things that sets the inexperienced songwriters and producers apart from the seasoned professionals is the effective use of contrast. A novice songwriter can have a great idea for a song, but it won't have the desired effect on the listener if the parts are not playing off of each other's differences. The melody in the verse and chorus might be in the exact same range (check out the chapter Modulation to learn a cure for this), the rate at which the chords change might be the same throughout the song, and so on.

Whether you're in a songwriting/composing, production or mixing phase, you need to know how to create contrast. Why is contrast so important? Mainly for two reasons, that really are kind of the same.

First, without contrast you'll have very little variation and therefore find it harder to maintain the listener's attention. And, related to this, without contrast your parts will lose a lot of their impact on the listener.

A good analogy for a song is a movie: the adrenaline-inducing action scenes need the mellower scenes before them, otherwise they just aren't as exciting. Also, every scene and transition needs to make sense and move the story along.

Contrast in Mixing

A powerful chorus with a powerful bass, banging drums, and sparkly top end will not sound very exciting if your verse has all those things in the same amounts.

Contrast can also be happening in the same part of the song, at the same time. Contrast then exists between the sounds that make up the complete mix. Two guitars, or two synth parts playing at the same time, usually benefit from having some distinct differences. One could have a generous amount of reverb while the other has a short delay and a subtle tremolo happening. One could be bright and full frequency while the other part is filtered to have a duller, darker sound.

You can create contrast by using several different-sounding reverbs in a track. This can be further enhanced with EQ; to create more dimension and contrast in a mix, let the short reverbs be bright and the long ones dark or vice versa.

Speaking of reverb, use different amounts of reverb for verse and chorus, and different lengths as well. A big emotional chorus can do with longer reverbs that could contrast with the tighter-sounding verses.

Play around with the opposites bright/dark and see what else you can come up with in terms of contrast in your mixing.

Contrast in Composition

In composition we have three elements to work with (possibly four if we count structure as its own entity): melody, harmony and rhythm.

Let's start with the main character in composition – the melody. Writing melodies with contrasts is essential for effective songwriting. One common way to do it is to change the melodic range between the verse and the chorus. Usually the melody in the chorus contains higher notes than the verse melody. The hook or song title (if vocals are used) often contains the highest note of the whole song.

The rhythm or length of the notes can also change in different sections of the song. If the verse contains lots of eighth-notes and a staccato feel to the melody, the chorus may have longer, more legato-like melodies. Or, as always, vice versa.

Phrasing is a really powerful tool that is sometimes overlooked in composition. If you always start your melody lines on the first beat of the measure, try contrasting that by starting on the second beat or between the downbeats.

Also, melodies don't need to start in the first measure and end in the last in a four- or eight-bar section. You can end a melodic phrase after three measures and start a new one in the fourth and so on. Listen to the song Do I Wanna Know by Arctic Monkeys for some cool ideas for less predictable phrasing. Try not to start all your melodic phrases on the same note, especially if that note is the tonic of the key (the note C in C major).

Harmonic contrast can be created by changing the harmonic rhythm – the number of chords per measure. Increasing the number of chords played per measure is an effective way to create the feeling of increased intensity just before the chorus hits, for example.

Introducing major chords in a section when mostly minor chords have been played in previous sections can have a lot of impact. Of course, make sure it fits the mood of the lyrics, if there are any.

Introducing four-note chords, when you've only used triads before, can create some subtle or not-so-subtle contrast.

Changing time signature in the chorus is a pretty extreme technique, but sometimes just what's needed. The Beatles' tune Lucy in the Sky With Diamonds uses 6/8 time in the verses while the chorus is recorded in straight 4/4.

The opposites sparse/dense can be used a lot when working with the arrangement part of a composition or production. Having the drums enter in the first chorus or second verse and having everything before that being very sparse can have great impact.

Vocal arrangements are great for this sort of contrast. Letting the vocal melody be carried by a single voice without doubles in the verse and going at it with multiple doubles and a wall of harmonies in the chorus is a tried and true technique.

Tip Number 34. Three Tricks to Give Your Chorus More Impact

Three subtle automation tricks you can do to enhance the impact of a section in your song, most commonly the chorus:

1. Automate the master fader to go up 1–2 dB when the chorus hits. Back it down again when the verse comes in. Another way to do it is to bring up the fader for the beginning of the chorus to get the impact and then back it off slowly after a bar or so.

2. On your master bus, insert an EQ that has a gentle shelving filter cutting a dB or two in the low bass. When the chorus hits, simply bypass the EQ and let the bass be just a little bit fuller. You can even do it on the top end as well, this way the chorus will have slightly more lows and highs and really sound big and powerful. It's all in the contrast!

3. You can emulate what happens when musicians play together and go up in tempo slightly in the chorus and outros, etc. When the chorus hits, go up one or two BPM to get a bit more energy, contrast and life to your arrangement.

Tip Number 35. Vocal Harmony Contrast Trick

Vocal harmonies can take up a lot of space in a mix; often you'd want to double, triple, quadruple (etc.) each part and you'll end up with a lot of tracks. Before it's time to mix you're doing yourself a favor if you mix all the harmony vocal tracks down to a single stereo track.

When doing this, a good idea is to make different versions for different parts of your song. You'll often want to build the track so that the biggest climax comes in the last chorus.

More high-frequency content often equals more excitement, so start by doing a mix where the high harmonies are allowed to dominate a bit. This is for the last chorus. Then make at least one different mix where the low and mid harmonies take the lead role.

If you have harmony vocals in the verses too, do similar contrasting parts for them. Be creative, experiment.

Tip Number 36. Vocal Chorus Lift

These are some simple yet effective techniques to make your vocals have impact in the chorus. They both use the element of contrast to some degree.

1. Duplicate the vocal track and compress the new track hard. Use some sort of distortion or amp emulation and process the vocal heavily. In the chorus, blend in the processed track subtly with the original for some impact and energy.

2. Use a 1/4 note delay in the verse and change to a 1/2 note delay in the chorus, with the feedback turned up slightly. This will give the vocal a lot of depth in the chorus; use EQ to cut out some of the high end of the delays to make them less noticeable.

Tip Number 37. The Pink Noise Trick

Pink noise is basically randomized hiss that has the same amount of energy in every octave of the frequency spectrum. The perhaps better known type of noise, white noise, has equal amounts of energy for every frequency.

Since the octaves (double the frequency number to go up one octave) in the treble region have more frequencies in them, compare 5000–10 000 Hz with 50–100 Hz; it sounds like there is more energy in the top end than in the low end.

Pink noise therefore sounds more balanced and represents the whole frequency spectrum better to the human ear. One use for pink noise in a mix is where you need to increase the energy in a section. You can sneak it in there to fill out the frequency spectrum and add power.

You can also use white noise or simply EQ the low end out of the pink noise. Listen to the Beatles track I Want You (She's So Heavy) to hear the effect. Lennon apparently used the white noise generator on a Moog synthesizer for that track.

THE LOW END –

GET IT RIGHT

G etting the low end right seems kind of like the Holy Grail of mixing these days. It can absolutely be tricky to get the low end right; there is so much energy down there that you have to tame, and this part of the frequency spectrum is where the acoustic problems in your room really reveal themselves.

The low end is also probably what has changed the most in the frequency spectrum if you compare modern mixes to the ones of yesteryear. Just think about where the kick drum used to live in the mixes from the 1960s and 1970s: the kick drum usually has its fundamental energy in the 100–120 Hz area. In a modern pop or hip hop production, the kick drum would be down at 50–60 Hz a lot of the time – that's a whole octave lower!

The same could be said for the bass, which is often a sub bass-heavy synth bass in modern productions, so we now have an octave of extra energy that needs to have room to live in our mixes…

First of all, professionally mixed and mastered tracks usually have far less bass than most people tend to think. Referencing some well-mixed music, in more or less the same genre as your own, in a well-treated room or through headphones that have a realistic representation of the low end is good starting point, as is using a spectrum analyzer and having a look at those reference tracks.

Getting used to seeing how the energy is distributed across the frequency spectrum, in productions you like the sound of, gives you a great tool for keeping an eye on your own productions. It allows you to see those little red flags when something may be off with your frequency balance.

Tune Up

Before you touch any EQ I would suggest you check the tuning of your kick drum. Use a spectrum analyzer, a tuner or Melodyne if you like, to determine the pitch of the kick drum. I'm assuming now that you are using samples or synthesized drums; if you're using a recording of an acoustic drum kit, this can still be relevant if want to fill out the bottom end of your kick drum with a triggered sample or sub tone (see Tip Number 42). If it's a mid-heavy drum sample, make sure you find the low frequency peak and check what frequency it's at.

First, make sure that the kick drum isn't just generally out of tune, i.e. sitting somewhere between two semitones. Fine-tune it manually using a pitch shift tool or use Melodyne or Auto-Tune to get it spot on the closest note.

The next step is to determine if the note in question is a good note to have in the low end of your arrangement. The note should be in the key of the song and it should be one of the main notes of the scale, like the first, the fifth or perhaps the third. If you're unsure, look at what notes the bass is playing, listen to the kick and bass together, and tune the kick so that there is a minimum of clashing happening between those two elements.

The Kick Drum

A modern kick drum sound really consists of several elements. You have the initial transient, which is heard as the attack of the sound; this will happen in the mids and possibly upper mids of the frequency spectrum.

The part that (hopefully) will hit you in the chest when heard on a decent size system will have its main energy around 80–120 Hz.

The body (low frequencies) of the kick usually has a much longer decay time than the higher frequencies of the kick drum. The main energy will usually be around 50 or 60 Hz, although it can go down to around 40 Hz in some cases (energy that low will not be heard on a lot of smaller-sized systems and would need lots of harmonics to be represented well).

One thing to keep in mind is the length of the kick drum in relation to the perceived low end. The low frequencies need more time to be perceived than the higher frequencies, partly because they are more felt than heard.

This means that if you make the kick drum shorter, especially if you make it a lot shorter, the low end will have less impact and the kick drum will be heard overall as having less bottom end.

Layering Kick Drum Samples

A lot of the kick drum samples found in modern sample libraries have all the qualities mentioned above in differing amounts, but these elements can also function as a guide when layering several samples to create your own composite kick drum sample.

You can find samples that complement each other –perhaps one that is a low bass-heavy sample, while the other has a mid-frequency knock, etc. Alternatively, you can use samples that are more similar and just filter out all the parts you don't need in each sample.

Even if you go for the first alternative, you will probably have to do some filtering to prevent too much build-up and masking of some frequencies (see the section "Frequency Masking" for more details).

Other alternatives when it comes to layering are using a recorded acoustic drum layered with samples to provide the elements you're lacking; or you can use samples (or again, a recorded performance) and layer with a synth part. See Tip Number 38 for more details on this technique.

Mono or Stereo?

Back in the days when most music ended up on vinyl, the low bass had to be in mono since stereo information down in the lower frequencies would make the needle jump out of the groove.

In the digital age (disregarding the recent vinyl revival for now) there are still reasons to keep your bass in mono:

1. Bass frequencies have a lot of energy (they move lots of air) and will take up more space in a mix than mid or high frequencies. Keeping the bass mono will limit the amount of space used.

2. Most subwoofers are mono anyway so you'll have more control over the sound being played back on different systems if you keep the bass in mono.

3. Stereo information might very well mean phase problems when the left and right channels combine (in a mono speaker or in the phantom center between two speakers). Bass frequencies are sensitive to phase problems and can easily lose punch and definition.

What if you like the sound of bass in stereo? Don't worry, the human brain can't localize sound at frequencies lower than about 80 Hz.

This means that there's no real benefit in having frequencies down there panned out in stereo anyway, so you can concentrate on higher frequencies giving your bass that stereo spread. There are a couple of ways to do this.

If the bass you're using contains stereo information, duplicate the track and put an EQ/filter on each track. On the first track, put a low pass filter at 80 Hz. Use your best-quality EQ for this to avoid excessive phase distortion.

Now make this track mono; you can sum the left and right channel to mono and you can separate the channels into two mono tracks. This will give you three tracks to compare; choose the one that sounds the best to you in terms of punch, clarity, etc. On the duplicated track, use a high pass filter starting at 80 Hz. Go higher with the filter and find the sweet spot where you get rid of some mud but still feel that the bass sound is perceived as one sound.

When the sound source is in mono you have to create the stereo width. Do exactly as in the previous example but instead of "monoizing" the low part, you make the higher frequencies stereo by adding chorus or delaying the left or right channel and adding a subtle pitch shift to either side. Make sure it sounds alright in mono too!

You can also send a mono bass sound to a short reverb, and filter out everything below 200 Hz on the reverb send.

Tip Number 38. Sine Tone Bass Double

To get a more solid bottom end in your mix, it can be a good idea to take complete control of the low low end. Sometimes the lowest part of the frequency spectrum of your mix is the kick drum. In that case, try Tip Number 42 (Gated Sub Bass Sine Wave).

When the bass is your main player, you might want to make sure everything's alright down there. One thing you can do is to make sure that everything below around 150 Hz is completely in mono. Our ears don't have the capacity to discern the direction of a sound that low in frequency anyway. There are several tools for this job, but a simple EQ with MS function works well. Just high pass the "side" channel and you're good.

If you want to get even more control than that, you can filter out the fundamental (the lowest and biggest bump on the spectrum analyzer) and duplicate the MIDI notes onto a new track, then let a pure sine wave double the original bass.

Tip Number 39. Synth Bass Accents and Ghost Notes Using Gates

This is a great technique when you're using long synth bass notes that are somewhat static in nature; but it also works any time you want to add accents or ghost notes to a bass or synth part or even a white noise-type sound.

Duplicate the track to which you want to add the accents. On the duplicate track, insert a gate. Open up a MIDI track, write out notes where you want the accents. A good starting point for trying this out is to have a note on beat one and three and some eighth-note triplets on beat four.

On the MIDI track, load up a snappy kick drum sample and turn down the channel fader so that no sound is heard from the kick drum. Choose the MIDI channel as key input on the gate and let the gate close completely when it isn't being triggered by the kick drum. The duplicate track should now only be heard when the gate is being opened by the kick drum. When listening to this in solo you're hearing the accents and ghost notes only.

Turn down the fader of the duplicate track and listen to the original as you slowly turn up the fader until the accents are heard and sound balanced in the mix.

Tip Number 40. Kick Drum Knock Parallel Trick

Duplicate your kick drum track. On the second track, put a compressor with a 30–50 millisecond attack and a long release. Compress the track hard! Blend it in with the original kick drum track and listen to how the enhanced transient gives your kick drum a great knock that will cut through the mix.

While listening to both tracks blended together, use a high pass filter after the compressor and go up to the point where the low end is clear but stop before the knock gets to thinned out and weak. You can also try boosting with a bell curve, sweeping through the mids until you find a nice presence that fits the mix.

Tip Number 41. Manipulating Low End Through Kick Drum Length

By shortening a kick drum, you will change the perceived amount of low end that kick drum has. This technique can be used to give more impact to a section of a song.

For instance, imagine you shorten the kick drum in the verses, either by editing the waveform directly or by using a gate that closes after a number of milliseconds.

When the chorus hits, you simply revert to the longer version of the kick or turn the gate off in the latter example. This will get you more impact and perceived low end without you doing any EQ changes in the low end that might affect processing like compression, limiting and so on.

Tip Number 42. Gated Sub Bass Sine Wave

If you have a punchy and good sounding kick drum that is lacking a little low end, there is a simple but very effective trick that you can use without having to struggle with phase and excessive filtering like you might when layering different samples to create a perfect full-frequency kick drum.

On a new track, have a low sine tone play constantly. Make sure it's in the key of the song so that it clashes minimally with the bass and other instruments. Insert a gate on the sine wave track and have the kick drum open the gate to let the sine wave through. Experiment with the hold and release parameters of the gate to find a length of the bass note that fits the track.

Tip Number 43. Low End Parallel Kick Drum Trick

Duplicate the kick drum track. Put a compressor with slow attack (around 30 ms) and long release on it, and compress it fairly hard. Now there shouldn't be much sustain to the sound, there should be a clear attack and not much else. You can also use a transient designer for this, turning back the sustain and adding some attack.

Now use an EQ to boost the low end generously after the compressor. You can use a Pultec-style EQ here and boost around 100 Hz or lower and turn the attenuate knob up to attenuate the frequencies just above where you're boosting. This is sometimes referred to as the Pultec trick. A DBX 160 was usually used as the compressor when this was done back in the day.

Tip Number 44. The Bass Phase Trick

Sometimes you're dealing with a bass sound that you find difficult to EQ. There might be many frequencies that either mask other elements of the mix or just sound bad to your ear. At such times you usually end up with a pretty crazy-looking EQ curve with lots of really deep cuts and a few boosts in between.

One thing you can try in such a situation is a little bit more extreme than what you achieve with normal EQ:

1. Duplicate the bass track and reverse the phase (polarity) of the original track. There should now be complete silence when you play back the two tracks together. An EQ is essentially messing with phase in order to cut frequencies so what you have achieved here is basically one giant cut across all frequencies.

In order for the total phase cancellation to work, both tracks must have the same volume and the exact same processing inserted. Therefore it's a good idea to route both tracks to an aux and do all the processing there.

2.Since the phase cancellation relies on both signals being exactly the same, you can now start creating differences by manipulating the frequencies on the first track. Try bosting 50 Hz slightly with a bell curve and you'll notice that only this frequency will be heard (cutting actually works here too since that will create a difference in the same way, but boosting is definitely more intuitive).

Tip Number 45. 808 Basslines

Perhaps the most famous drum machine kick drum of them all, the 808, can also be used as a bass instrument to great effect.

Choose a sample with a long sustain. Make sure it's in tune, either by tuning it manually while checking a tuner or using a tool like Melodyne.

Load up the sample into a sampler and adjust the root note so that you'll get a C note when pressing the C on the MIDI keyboard. Make sure you adjust the settings to make the notes cut each other off when played. Get a bit of release going to get a more natural sound. Adjust the attack to be as soft or as punchy as you like.

Some 808 samples already has a lot of distortion on them, but you may need to add a bit of your own distortion to make the notes be heard in the mid-range of the mix. Guitar amp emulations are great for this when used in parallel.

EQING WITHOUT EQ

WITHOUT EQ

[... AND THE ART OF ARRAN-GEMENT]

E qualization is probably the most common type of processing in audio engineering. It is that for a reason: when we're trying to fit a big number of tracks together without it all sounding like a muddy mess, we're bound to be eliminating some parts of it, while accentuating other parts. This we usually do with equalization.

But there can be prices to pay when EQing becomes the fix-all solution for fitting a large number of sounds together. What an equalizer does is basically messing with the phase of a signal. While this is necessary for it to do its job, it can also cause unwanted and unpleasant artifacts, especially when there are many instances of equalizers doing some heavy lifting in a mix.

EQing too boldly can cause a mix to sound lifeless and without power. There are other methods to consider before you reach for an EQ every time. Of course, sometimes EQ is the best option, alone or used together with these other techniques.

Basic Tools

The part of the frequency spectrum where the bass lives is especially sensitive to phase degradation and can lose clarity and punch quickly if too much is done to it.

I would suggest starting with the volume fader. If the mix sounds too bassy, too muddy or too harsh, turn down the bassy, muddy or mid-rangy tracks a bit. Sounds simplistic, maybe, but it is too easily forgotten. By doing it this way you don't do any unnecessary digital processing to the sound and you preserve all that's good about it.

"Carving" is a term that often comes up when equalization is discussed. It usually means attenuating certain frequencies of a sound to make room for another sound when they're being heard at the same time.

Although this technique might be just what the doctor ordered, simply panning some of the sounds away from each other in the stereo field might do the trick.

Arrangement Issues

Arrangement is something that is generally overlooked by a lot of bands and novice producers. Arrangement is a deep subject and it can mean a number of things. The American Federation of Musicians defines it like this:

Arranging is the art of preparing and adapting an already written composition for presentation in other than its original form.

This might seem foreign to people producing electronic or sample-based music, as the writing, arranging, and producing usually takes place at the same time or are on-going processes that alternate.

Asking you the following two questions can get you some part of the way to understanding the role that arrangement plays in a complete production.

What space is each element of the arrangement inhabiting? What role does each element have when it comes to telling the story of the song?

The first question deals with how you place each instrument and vocal part rhythmically, harmonically and frequency-wise. There is a tendency among inexperienced producers and bands to have two guitars or several synths essentially playing the same rhythm in the same octave. This means that they are covering the same part of the frequency spectrum at the exact same time.

This usually gives you two problems. First, the arrangement gets muddy because there is a lot of frequency masking happening. Furthermore, if the music is performed by a band, as opposed to a DAW with pretty much an infinite amount of potential instrument parts, you use up the instruments that can be used for other, more effective things. Maybe more often than not then, what can seem like a normal part of the mixer's struggle is primarily an issue with lack of good arrangement. As mentioned, having multiple instruments playing chords in the same section of a song can get problematic, especially if they're not carefully arranged.

The first thing to make sure is that they're not playing in the same octave if they don't have to (that is, unless the sound you're after dictates that they do). If you do need to double parts in the same octave, working with differences in tone is often essential. In all other cases, have one of the parts play an octave above the other.

Alternatively, one part can be wrapped around the other, so that the lowest notes are played below the other instrument's notes and the rest of the notes are played above. Limiting the amount of notes played by each instrument can also help immensely.

Remember that the parts should complement each other to make a complete-sounding whole, not compete with each other for attention.

The other thing to look out for is where things are placed on the timeline of a track. Work with rhythms that complement each other, instead of just having all the chord-playing instruments playing the exact same rhythm. There is a good reason why so many dance music producers program the bass notes on the up beat so that they're never heard at the same time as the kick drum.

So, moving instruments out of each other's way frequency-wise and rhythmically will mean that the problem-solving approach is less necessary in mixing and will make the end result sound better and be more effective in grabbing the listener's attention.

The last aspect we'll consider here is the intent of the arrangement as the song evolves from intro to verse, from verse to chorus, etc. This is kind of a theatrical approach; you're building different scenes and the impact of one scene will be directly related to what the previous scene was like. If all the instruments are playing all the time, there is so much less room for surprising the listener and building suspense from the ground up.

Think about watching a play where all the actors are present on the stage throughout the whole play. It can work in a minimalist style, as it could in minimalist styles of music, but it is often a recipe for art that is not very dynamic or interesting.

Harmonics

Assuming that the arrangement is as good as it can be, or that you're polishing someone else's less-than-perfect production, let's dive in to some mixing tools to try when EQ might not be the perfect option.

Harmonic distortion is an interesting tool. It can create or raise the amplitude of harmonic overtones related to the fundamental pitch of a sound.

Hearing harmonics related to the fundamental is actually enough for your brain to figure out what the pitch of the sound is and recreate it so that you think you're hearing it, even if it's filtered out.

An example of this is a telephone conversation. The frequency range of the microphone and speaker of a telephone is limited to such an extent that the actual pitch of our voice (the fundamental frequency) is not being transmitted. But still you're experiencing the pitch of the voice of the person at the other end of the line.

This illusion is called "the missing fundamental". With this is mind, there are good reasons to distort your bass lines and kick drums. This way they will be heard on smaller speakers that can't represent the lowest part of the frequency spectrum. It will also help a lot with making your bass cut through the mix without crazy EQ. You're essentially moving the energy of the track up to the higher frequencies.

Distortion might affect the sub frequencies, however, so it might be a good idea to split your bass track to two tracks, and have one with the frequencies below somewhere around 60–100 Hz filtered out. Distort that track and leave the track containing the sub bass frequencies untouched. As always, experiment.

As for the top end, distortion can do a lot for you there as well. It can give an instrument a organic sort of presence in the upper mids and high end if used with caution and taste.

Again, by splitting your track into two separate tracks and inserting a low pass filter on one and a high pass filter on the other, you can gently distort the top end of a track without affecting the low end, or vice versa.

Time for Attack

An often-overlooked aspect of compression is the effect on the frequencies of a sound. By adjusting the attack of a compressor you can affect the amount of brightness you'll end up with. The reason for this is that most of the brightness we perceive is due to what the transients sound like. The tail of a sound is much less important to our brain in this regard.

How do you go about it then? Well, if you compress a sound with a slow attack and a fairly slow release you will have more of the fast transient coming through and thus you'll have more perceived brightness. Adjusting the attack to a faster attack time, let's say 3 milliseconds, will darken the sound substantially.

If you own a transient designer (which you should, it's not a secret if you read this book that they are one of my absolute favorite tools), you can simply adjust the attack to get a similar effect. Turn up the attack for more brightness and vice versa.

At the Source

If you're recording the sounds yourself, the absolute best way to EQ something is to move the microphone around until you get more of what you need or less of what you don't want.

There are guidelines to be found regarding specific sources. Pointing a microphone directly at the cone of a guitar amplifier will get you more treble than pointing it slightly to the side of the cone. Tilting the mic slightly down towards the chest of a vocalist will get you more bottom end and "chestiness", etc.

When using two microphones at the opposite sides of a sound source, like the top and bottom mic on a snare drum or one mic in front and one behind an acoustic piano or a guitar amplifier, switching the polarity of one of the microphones is the most powerful EQ.

Generally, when using multiple microphones, the 3:1 (three to one) rule is a good starting point. The idea of the 3:1 rule is that if you mic up a source and have another microphone near that microphone, the second microphone should be at least three times the distance from the first mic that the first mic is from the source.

So if you have a mic one foot from a source, the nearest mic should be at least three feet from the first microphone. The reason for this is that the difference in amplitude from the sound source going into the first microphone is so much higher than the amplitude going into the second mic, therefore the out-of-phase signal from the second mic is so low that it won't make any serious damage.

Bright Spaces

Sometimes adding a bright sound instead of brightening the sounds that are there already can be a great idea. Turning up the hi-hat track or adding a shaker can add some much-needed brightness to a song. Letting the reverb or delay be a little bright instead of cranking up the highs of the dry sound can also be a trick that ends up working better in the mix.

So, next time you reach for the EQ, spend a minute or two thinking about other ways to go first.

Tip Number 46. The Natural Arrangement

All musical instruments produce composite tones, consisting of many pure tones, called harmonics, produced simultaneously

This is a quote from Harvard Dictionary of Music. All tonal instruments have harmonics (the exception is the sine tone). The harmonics follow a certain pattern, which can be seen below. The picture depicts 16 harmonics that belong to a C note. Different instruments will produce these harmonics with different amplitude for each harmonic – this is a big part of timbre and explains why a saxophone sounds so different from a recorder.

What's interesting is that the harmonic series is an arrangement in itself; take a look at the spacing between the notes. The low notes are pretty wide apart and that distance gets more and more narrow when we go up the scale. Use this as a guideline when arranging notes in chords or between different instruments in a song.

The amplitude between the harmonics also resemble a complex arrangement, with most of the energy down low, getting more and more subtle as we go up the frequency range.

Tip Number 47. The Small Speaker Test

Working on a monitor speaker that can represent the whole frequency range is essential in mixing since you need to hear all the details in order to make the right decisions.

But when all the little tweaking is done, using a small speaker that has a limited frequency bandwidth and is possibly more on the low-resolution side can be a great idea.

What should you be listening for on a small speaker? Well, you tend to hear what's going on in the mid-range pretty well since there is not a lot of bottom or top end to distract you. And also, a speaker with a single driver will have no phase distortion between the woofer and the tweeter.

Listen to the levels of the main things like kick, snare and vocals. Is something poking out too much? Is there frequency masking happening?

Can you hear the kick and bass well enough? If not, consider adding some distortion and/or mid-range EQ.

The legendary producer Quincy Jones used small Auratone speakers to see if the mix still had vibe. The theory was that if the mix sounded great on those, it would sound great practically everywhere.

Tip Number 48. Kick and Bass Muting Test

This is a very useful technique for finding muddy frequencies in your mix and discovering frequency masking in the bass and low mids.

Some people swear by the practice of high pass filtering pretty much every track in your mix to prevent low-mid and bass build-up. Although there is some sense to this technique as it can prevent a muddy or overly bassy mix, it can also leave your mix sounding thin and lacking in warmth.

A simple technique that relies on your ears instead of dogmatic ideas is to mute your bass tracks and your kick drum tracks and listen to all the other elements of your mix to hear if there is a substantial amount of energy down in the bass. If so, locate the tracks that are responsible for this energy and filter some of it out.

Synth pads are notorious for containing low end energy that might not be obvious but will eat up lots of space and compete with your bass and kick drum.

Unmute the kick and bass and listen to the difference in definition and punch. Try filtering out some more and see if it improves the low end or if you're starting to lose some fullness of the mix.

Tip Number 49. Hunt for Frequency Masking

Since similar frequencies have a tendency to mask each other, one approach is to go on a hunt for masking that may occur in your mix. This is the same kind of thing that were covered in the previous tip "Kick and Bass Muting Test", but this time we'll go for the whole frequency spectrum.

Mute different tracks that have their main frequencies in common. Listen to what happens to the vocals when you mute the synth pads, guitars, piano, etc . Focus your listening on specific frequency ranges. Do the vocals get more air (super high frequencies) when the buzzy synth or piano is muted? How about the presence frequencies 2–5 kHz?

When you find a problem, attack it with regular EQ (cutting out a bit of the frequencies that clash from one of the offending tracks), side-chain compression, or dynamic EQ.

Check out "The Multitrack Side-chaining Trick" for a technique you can use to remedy masking.

Tip Number 50. Reverb Harmony Trick

This is similar to the Reverb Exciter Trick (Tip Number 14), but instead of pitching the sound up one octave, you do a harmony like a 3rd, 5th or 6th above the note that is being played.

Using the same instrument or a different one, add a new track to your arrangement and play a harmony line above the original lead sound. Insert a reverb and adjust it so that it's 100% wet. Blend the reverb track subtly with the dry track.

Tip Number 51. The ABBA Varispeed Trick

ABBA's engineer Michael Tretow had a love for experimentation in the studio. He used to wrap adhesive tape around the capstan in order to change the size of it slightly. That way the speed would be changed a little bit, so when you recorded a track onto another track on the tape and played them back together you'd get some interesting phasing effects.

Another trick he was fond of was the varispeed trick. When recording vocals he would change the speed slightly and then adjust it back to normal. What this did is change the formants of the vocals. A formant is a cluster of harmonic overtones which make up the timbre of a sound.

This can be used as sound design in itself or mixed together with another take recorded without varispeed adjustments for a thicker, denser sound.

Another way this can be used is by recording drums at a slightly higher speed and lowering the speed back to normal. This gives the drums a subtle thickening effect and weight.

So how do you achieve this in your DAW? Logic Pro has a varispeed feature that can be used for this. I personally love a tool like Melodyne for this task. It lets you manipulate the formants directly — lowering the formants equals recording to a higher tempo and slowing it down again. And vice versa.

WAYS TO "GLUE" A MIX

There are certain terms that seem to come up time and time again when mixing and music production is being discussed. Among those, "glue" is certainly one of the most common ones.

The problem with terms like these is that they can be quite vague and perhaps do not mean the same for all people (terms like "warmth" and "depth" seem especially problematic in this regard).

What this term means here is that the elements of a mix sound like they belong together, there is some unity being perceived and there is an organic relationship between the different instruments. Glue makes it sound more like a record and less like a collection of individual sounds.

There are basically two ways to achieve this quality: to preserve it or to create it.

Preserving the Glue

A recording of musicians playing together in a single space will have the maximum amount of glue. The musicians will react to each other's performance, and therefore all the tracks will affect each other.

In such a scenario the glue already exists and the most common way of removing that precious adhesive is to separate the frequencies too much. There is a fine balance between a muddy and unfocused mix and a glued and coherent mix.

You can certainly remove some of the magic of a mix by carving out too much space for each instrument. Like Bob Dylan said to Ed Cherney, listening to a mix of one of his songs, "You've fucked it up, you can hear everything."

Sometimes the space where the tracks were recorded was really non-reverberant, sometimes the space and the glue factor might not be very pronounced. In this case there are ways to create some glue where there is little or none.

Creating the Glue

There are some tried and true ways to inject some realistic glue into your production.

The three main tools used here are reverb, compression and EQ.

Create a Room

Create an aux with a reverb that will be the "room" where all the tracks are living. It can be a room, a hall or a plate reverb and the length can vary according to taste and general vision of the mix. Generally shorter reverbs are great for uptempo songs and longer reverbs work better for slower songs. The idea here is to send a little from most tracks to that one reverb to create unity in your mix.

Make the Sounds Move Together

Another way to create some glue is to use compression. The two main reasons that compression can create a sense of glue is that the dynamics of one instrument will affect the dynamics of the other tracks in your mix. This in itself will create the illusion that the tracks belong together and aren't just thrown together randomly.

Another reason is that a lot of compressors have non-linear qualities, distortion, going on; this will give the tracks a more uniform sound. Think about the use of a console, you get a little bit of distortion from each signal passing through the channel strip, every channel has the same model preamp, the same EQ, etc. A little bit of similar processing on several tracks goes a long way in creating a more uniform sound.

Bus compression is the way to go here, either on a sub-group like a drum bus or an instrument bus, or on the whole mix. A low ratio with medium attack and medium or auto release, doing 1–3 dB of gain reduction is a pretty safe practice when compressing the whole mix for glue.

If you're looking to enhance the groove of the song, try compressing harder (like a lot harder) with a faster attack and release; adjust the release until the compression is pumping in a groove that fits the song and back off on the gain reduction until it's more of a subtle enhancement (unless you're going for extreme effect, of course).

The Power of Noise

For a long time there has been a struggle for cleaner signal chains to achieve recordings with better signal-to-noise-ratio. In hindsight, however, we recognize that there is a certain glue that comes with analog recording equipment like multi-channel consoles and tape machines. A big part of that glue is due to noise, namely the mostly random analog hiss that is inevitable when you're working in the analog domain.

Noise has a tremendous power to glue different elements together, it does so by filling in those little spaces between the sounds just enough to create a sense of cohesiveness and depth. Instead of inserting a tape emulation that might add artifacts you don't actually want, a less intrusive way to get a bit of the glue that analog tape offered is to simply add some tape hiss to your mix, or specific tracks of your mix.

Tip Number 52. Drum Background Noise

A great way to add depth and variation to a drum loop is to add a background noise.

This technique is well suited for trip hop or downtempo productions as well as some kinds of hip hop and electronic music.

The noise could be an instrument with lots of sustain and an organic sort of sound; wind chimes are great for this. It can also be a found sound like ambient noise from a street, café, etc.

Make a one-bar loop of the noise and pitch shift until it sounds right. You can add processing like chorus and EQ to make the most out of this technique.

Tip Number 53. The Multitrack Side-Chaining Trick

When it comes to getting a mix to move, groove and feel alive, our most powerful tool is arguably volume automation. Side-chaining is a kind of volume automation, if you think about it, although it doesn't offer the flexibility of manual automation. It's still a super powerful tool, though.

Side-chaining is often used to avoid clashes between sounds that have similar frequency content, whether it be the bass getting out of the way of the kick drum or the mid-rangey guitars getting out of the way of the vocals. It can also be used to create a pumping sort of movement to the bass or the whole track.

This technique, however, is more about creating subtle movement across many tracks to make the mix seem more organic and less static. Insert compressors on several mid range-heavy instruments like synth pads and leads, percussive sounds, etc. Experiment with different routing, letting one or more track trigger the side chain on one track and find the combinations that seem to work.

Try to keep it simple, and be subtle with gain reduction; a couple of dB is often enough to make a difference.

Tip Number 54. Opposite Side Delay

A lot of times you want to keep certain tracks in your mix dry, so using reverb might not be an option. Still, keeping something completely dry can really make it sound like it's not part of the mix.

By having a delay that is panned to the opposite side of the dry sound, you get to keep the sound completely dry at one point in the stereo field while at the same time you get a sense of natural reflections elsewhere in the stereo field, which makes your brain accept it as being part of the space where the other sounds exist.

To make it less obvious to the ear, keep the feedback of the delay low. The delay time can be short like a slapback delay (80–120 ms) or longer; listen to what it does to the placement of your track in the space of your mix when adjusting the delay.

If you want to keep your dry sound panned center, use two delays, one panned hard left and the other hard right.

Let one of the delays be a little shorter, around 90 milliseconds or so, and the other around 120 milliseconds, both with the feedback turned down to zero.

DIFFERENT
KINDS OF
SPACE

The element of space is something that is absolutely vital in a sonically pleasing mix. Without any kind of space you'll end up with a two-dimensional soup where everything steps on everything else. It's often essential to master the element of space in order to make a mix or production sound engaging, interesting and "real", for lack of a better term.

Space in a mix can essentially mean two things. One is the separation between different sounds in the mix, the space between sounds. The other meaning of space refers to the third dimension of a mix, what some people call front-to-back panning, the space in front of and behind sounds.

Frequency Masking

The space between two separate sounds is the result of the overlapping of frequencies that is happening at any given time. This not only affects the perceived space between sounds, but also how much of the frequency spectrum of a specific sound will be audible to the listener. What comes into play here is the phenomenon of frequency masking.

Frequency masking is the psychoacoustic phenomenon that results in certain sounds not being heard due to other sounds blocking our perception. For this to occur, some conditions need to be fulfilled.

First, there needs to be sufficient amplitude; a really quiet sound will not be able to mask a much louder sound. Second, lower frequencies are much more effective at masking higher frequencies than vice versa.

Countering frequency masking is pretty much the basic task of EQing in a mix. There are other ways than EQ to fight destructive frequency masking, though. Take a look at the chapter "EQing Without EQ" for some other vital techniques.

If mono compatibility is not a major concern of yours, you can solve a lot of the masking by panning your sounds so that they're distributed across the stereo field in a manner in which they don't overlap too much. In my opinion, this works best in combination with some EQ and filtering, preferably done when you're listening to the mix in mono.

Front-To-Back

The second type of space we're talking about is the space in front of or behind a sound. This type of space determines where your brain will place a certain sound depth-wise.

There are a couple of ways to create the illusion of a sound being moved away from the listener. One way is simply volume manipulation; turning down the fader will make the sound appear less in your face and seem farther away.

Another way to place sounds closer or farther away from the listener without any use of reverb or delay is to manipulate the high end frequencies of the sounds. Using a shelving-filter and attenuating the high frequencies of a sound will make it sound like it's coming from further back in the mix.

Reverb and Delay

Before simply slapping a reverb on your tracks, there are a few things that are valuable to keep in mind.

Really short reverbs (under one second) will make a sound bigger by giving it a bit of aura. The same can be achieved with short stereo delays (keep the feedback to a minimum).

Long reverbs and long delays will move a sound back in the mix.

Make sure to EQ your reverbs and delays when needed. This usually means cutting out some of the lows and some of the extreme highs. And don't be afraid to do surgical EQ when there is some annoying resonance in the mids, or you simply want to bend the reverb into whatever shape your vision of the mix dictates.

Cutting out the high end might make the reverb too hard to hear in a busy mix. Adding in a de-esser, dynamic EQ or multi-band compressor that reacts to the spitty and sibilant frequencies that are fed into it will let you have a bright reverb without it sounding like a cocaine-induced 1980s mix.

A sparse mix can usually handle longer reverbs and can benefit from it since the tails will fill up the gaps and glue the tracks together nicely. This is doubly true if the tempo is slow. In a busier mix shortening the reverbs can be a good idea.

If a sound seems to lose too much urgency or intelligibility, turn up the pre-delay to allow for a bit of dry signal to pass through before the reverb enters. If you go too far it will sound like a slapback echo.

It might be a good idea to insert a delay before the reverb instead of using the pre-delay on your reverb. There are to reasons to do this; the first is that you have a musical value like a sixteenth-note or an eighth-note on your delay instead of milliseconds that are used on most reverbs.

The second reason is that you have full control over when the reverb kicks in so you can let the dry signal through for as long as you like. A pre-delay on a reverb might do different things to the early reflections and the tail, you really don't have any control over the algorithms.

Impulse response reverbs (aka convolution reverbs) are great for realistic spaces. Algorithmic reverbs are great for reverb tails and sound design.

Having a reverb that receives a bit of signal from most of the tracks will help create a uniform sound and create a bit of glue.

Plate reverbs are great for creating depth and space without giving the impression of a big hall or actual room. Plates are also good for creating a vintage vibe.

Spring reverb is the plate reverb's less-fancy cousin. It can work great for the same reasons as the plate. It does sound less refined and polished and can sound boingy, especially on drums. Cutting out a lot of the low frequencies can help a lot. Mono spring and plate reverbs can sound really cool on vocals.

Tip Number 55. Manipulating the Stereo Field

We know that what we perceive as stereo is basically the difference between the left and the right channel. One way to increase this difference is to manipulate the polarity of a sound, this means that the wave form is turned upside down so that the plus side of the wave becomes minus and vice versa.

The first technique you can use is to duplicate a stereo track, invert the channels so that the left channel is now the right channel and vice versa. Flip the polarity on the duplicate track and blend this channel subtly with the original track. The more you use of the polarity-inverted track, the wider the stereo image will appear; but if you go too far you will have unnatural-sounding frequency holes in your mix and it will sound bad when collapsed to mono.

Another way to do it is to set up speaker emulations on two mono auxes and flip the polarity on both of them. Pan them hard left and right and send a bit of your track to both auxes.

Tip Number 56. Cascading Delays

You can create really cool textures and depth by creating cascading delay chains. This is basically one delay going into another delay and then another one if required.

Try having a 1/2 note delay going into a 1/8 note triplet delay, then reverse the chain and let the triplet delay go into the slower delay; it's quite a different sound.

Make this technique really interesting by having different EQ curves on the different delays and process them creatively using distortion, guitar amp emulation, chorus, phaser, or whatever you can come up with.

Try panning them differently to increase separation and create some stereo movement. Experiment with different amounts of send to each delay.

Tip Number 57. Double Reverb Depth Trick

This is a trick that can achieve a more interesting depth to a sound. This is done by giving a different texture to different parts of the frequency spectrum for a given sound.

Create two reverb sends. Put an EQ in front of each of the two reverbs. The first EQ will have a bandpass filter spanning from, let's say, 250 Hz to 2000 Hz. The other EQ will have a high pass filter, filtering out everything below 2000 Hz. Cut out some of the extreme highs if you desire.

Use different algorithms for the two reverbs, and more importantly different reverb times. You can let the band-passed reverb be long and modulated while the bright reverb is just a short burst. Adjust the reverb sends until you get a good balance of the two reverbs for your mix.

If you want to get more width in your mix, do the same as above but pan the reverbs hard left and right.

Tip Number 58. The Abbey Road Reverb Trick

At the famous Abbey Road studio in London there has long been a practice of treating reverb that quite a few successful mixers have taken to heart to this day.

The idea behind this technique is to make the reverb blend into the mix, creating depth without being too noticeable. It also does wonders in making less-than-great-sounding algorithms sound more "expensive".
Start by inserting an EQ before the reverb on your aux channel. Roll off everything below 600 Hz. With a low pass filter, cut out everything over 10 kHz. Now you have reverb that won't clutter your low end and will not poke out in the high end and call too much attention to itself. Listen to the Wham! track Wake Me Up Before You Go Go to get an idea of how it can sound when you have too much top end in your reverbs.

What you can also do is to dip a little bit in the "presence" frequency range of your sound source. For vocals, attenuating your reverb send slightly at 3–4 kHz will make sure that the reverb isn't competing for attention in the area where the vocals have a lot of energy.

You can also go a lot lower with the low pass filter, especially on drums and other percussive instruments.

Tip Number 59. How to Move a Sound Back 50 Yards

Reverb is sometimes referred to as front-to-back panning, because you're creating the illusion of the dry sound being placed in a physical space and the louder you hear the reflections of that space in relation to the sound source, the farther away the sound source seems to your brain.

The problem is that when the sound source is far away from you, certain things happen to that sound while traveling to your eardrums. Simply using a close-miked sound, lowering the volume and adding loads of reverb will not account for what's happening in a real physical space. Here's how to get a tad more realism.

Reduce the lows and highs with EQ – those are the frequencies that don't make it that far compared to the mid frequencies. Use a compressor with a low ratio and let the threshold go all the way down or close to it. This will simulate how the air will compress sound when the sound is traveling a long distance.

Lastly, use a convolution reverb and select an impulse response that corresponds to the space you're trying to create. This technique works especially well when you want the illusion of a sound being heard outside, in a field or forest, for instance,

Tip Number 60. Transient Design Your Room

Transient designers can be used to change the size of the room in which something's been recorded. By turning up the sustain, the room will appear bigger. This is great for drum recordings where you want to give the illusion of a big room.

Similar result can be had by compressing the room sound, but using a transient designer is super-simple and precise and doesn't cause as many artifacts. Having said that, sometimes you want the artifacts of pumping compression.

Going the opposite direction, you can tighten up a room and make it punchy by reducing the sustain and increasing the attack slightly.

Tip Number 61. Clean Up Voice Recordings

A lot of times voice recording or instrument recordings are made in a less-than-perfect acoustic environment. Similar to the "Transient Design Your Room" tip above, you can use a transient designer to reduce the amount of room in a recording.

Simply back off on the sustain; this will decrease bad sounding early reflections and reverb tails. If you don't have a transient designer (I would strongly advise you to get one) you can get similar results by using a compressor with slow attack and slow release, used lightly.

Tip Number 62. Funnel Reverb

This is a simple but cool sounding technique that can be great on wide stereo sounds or mono sounds that have some sort of stereo effect like a stereo delay or chorusing.

You will need a reverb that sounds great in mono. For this I usually prefer a reverb with a more old-school sound like a plate or spring reverb.

You simply send your stereo track to a reverb that is panned center and has 0% width, i.e. completely mono.

This will give the impression of the sound going into a tunnel in the middle of the mix in a sort of funnel-shaped fashion.

Tip Number 63. Create Your Own Space Echo

The Space Echo tape delay is a legendary effect which has left a huge footprint in genres such as dub and various psychedelic and electronic sub-genres. This technique is inspired by this unit, but leaves endless room for innovation and experimentation.

This tutorial uses Ableton Live as an example of how to create this effect. However, these techniques can be applied to any DAW. If you're using Logic, for instance, you will use buses to send the signal to aux tracks and create the same kind of feedback loop as described below.

In Ableton, the buffer size (latency) might affect the time it takes for the audio to travel from one return track to another; so set the buffer to the lowest value your system can handle. You can always bounce your session to a stereo track and import into a new session where you create the space echo, print the delay tails, and import them back into your original session. This is good practice whenever you need to do CPU-intensive processing in a busy session.

Let's begin.

Create three return tracks: A, B and C. Enable send B on return track A and turn up the send. On return track B enable send C and turn it up. Finally, on return track C, enable send A and turn it up.

By sending any kind of audio to return track A (or any of the three return tracks, but for now let's stick to track A) we have now created a feedback loop: track A sends audio to track B, which in turn sends audio to track C, and track C sends audio back to track A etc.

Some caution is advised; the feedback can easily get out of control and result in distorting master buses, which in turn may damage your speakers and your ears! Adjust the levels of the sends and faders of the return/aux tracks until you get the desired level and length of the delay tail. Try this at low volume and always be prepared to pull down the fader on an overdriven track.

Now let's set up a basic space echo type effect. On track A, put a 16th note delay, 100% wet with 0% feedback. Try sending a snare to track A (turn down the sends slightly on all return tracks to avoid out-of-control self-oscillation) and listen to the result. A bit boring, but you get the idea.

Now let's get creative. Put an EQ on one of the tracks and filter out some of the high end, using a shelving filter or a high cut (low pass) filter. This way the signal will pass through this filter every time it passes through that particular return track, resulting in more top end being filtered out for each delay bounce. This emulates the way a tape delay loop sounds when the top end is starting to saturate and get more and more diminished.

To take the tape emulation a step further, place your favorite overdrive/saturation plugin on one of the tracks and listen to the delays get darker and more and more distorted. Get the amount of filtering and overdrive just right and the result is really quite beautiful in an old-school way.

The beauty of this technique is really the endless possibilities in designing your own sound. Try putting an EQ with a resonant peak on one of the tracks. Add a short reverb and set the dry/wet knob to somewhere between 1 and 10% (this works wonders for mono sounds; you'll hear a subtle space being created around the delay tail).

There is no end to the type of effects you can add to the chain (especially if they have a dry/wet knob so you can blend the effect in without it taking over completely): phasers, tremolos, delays (add another delay like the one you put on track A, this time to another one of the tracks and listen to the strange rhythms you can create) etc. You can also add more return tracks to make the chain even more complex.

Tip Number 64. De-esser Reverb Trick

This is a great way to mellow out reverbs to make them sit better in a mix. Insert a de-esser before your reverb on an aux (don't use this technique if you're using reverb with a dry/wet knob as an insert, as it will affect the dry signal).

You can push the de-esser a bit harder than you normally would, this will let you turn up the reverb more without it being too obvious or distracting. This is not only for vocals: try it on other instruments as well.

Tip Number 65. The Opposite EQ Widening Trick

If you have a mono instrument like a guitar or synthesizer there is a simple yet effective trick you can use to give it some width without messing with the phase at all. This is particularly great when you want your track to work well in mono.

Start by duplicating your track, panning each hard left and right, and inserting an EQ on both of the tracks. On one of the tracks find a suitable frequency to boost slightly and another frequency to attenuate.

On the other track you make the exact opposite EQ curve. Make sure you have the same frequency and Q-value on each of the filters and boost as many dBs as you attenuated on the other track and vice versa.

GROOVE

Whether you're programming your sounds or you're playing them live, finding a good groove and interesting rhythmic patterns is really important if you want to grab the listener. Groove is a part of the music that doesn't really hit our conscious mind, first and foremost. Getting the groove right will have people moving along to the music and make them feel the music in a pleasant way without really understanding why. Having a good groove is an effective way to capture the listener and make her stay till the end of the track.

Knowing the rhythmic basics like straight 8ths, 16ths, 8th note triplets and 16th note triplets is kind of a prerequisite for programming rhythmic parts. If you don't feel comfortable with those note values, go and learn them well before reading on.

Drums and Percussion

The rhythm section is arguably the backbone of most modern music production. After the vocals, the drums and percussion deserve the most focus, since they have the power to either make you tap your feet and nod your head or make your hands search for the next song or radio station.

Instead of using a groove template like an MPC-type swing, find the groove in your head, start feeling it in your body and use a MIDI controller to tap the beat with your hands and fingers. It won't be perfect, as it shouldn't, but manually moving things around after the fact will fix the mistakes and leave you with an alive and organic pattern that quantization and groove templates simply can't offer you. In the process, working to expand your rhythmic repertoire is something very worthwhile.

If you're not familiar with different kinds of swing, start by tapping out a shuffle rhythm with your hands on a table top or your knees. Shuffle is based on triplets instead of straight eighth-notes (each beat divided in perfect halves). Simply count 1-2-3 for each beat and replace the 2 with silence and let the 3 be the new 2. This gives you a long note and a short note for each beat.

Swing is a similar thing to shuffle but is less locked to the underlying triplets. This is harder and needs to be practiced before performed well since it relies on feel and having a good ear. Most DAWs have some sort of swing parameter in the MIDI section. Program a beat and let the hi-hat play straight eighth-notes. Adjust the swing parameter from extreme to subtle and learn to hear subtle differences, then practice playing the different swing patterns with your hands.

Polyrhythms

Practicing polyrhythms will take your rhythmic capability to the next level and will give you a natural feel for different kinds of triplets that can be used in a lot of places in music.

Polyrhythms are essentially two conflicting rhythms being played at the same time. Let's start with 3 over 2; the first beat of the two rhythms always happens at the same time. This means that three beats and two beats should last the exact same amount of time. That's always true for this kind of polyrhythm.

There are two basic ways to learn a particular polyrhythm, one is mathematical and the other one depends more on memorizing the sound.

Let's start with the first approach:

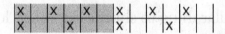

This is simple mathematics, you start by finding out the lowest common denominator of the two rhythms. In this case we have 3 and 2, so the lowest common denominator will be 6. Write out two rows with six boxes in each and put little Xs in each row, three in the top row and two in the bottom row. Make sure that the spacing between each of the Xs is the same for all the Xs that share the same row. You can now slowly count to six and tap the Xs with one of your hands for each row. Eventually you will get the hang of it and you no longer need to count to six; after practicing, you should be able to tap the polyrhythm with both hands while counting either of the two rhythms out loud. Now play it at double tempo and you have a 6 over 4 polyrhythm! This is especially good to know since the six beats in this case are basically quarter note triplets that you play over a 4/4 rhythm.

This technique can be applied to any polyrhythms. Try it with 5 over 4 and 4 over 3.

The second approach is to listen to a 3 over 2 polyrhythm and learn how it sounds. I find that using a phrase that has the same rhythm works great as a mnemonic. For 3 over 2, the phrase "It's very nice" works well. Sometimes you'll need to go through the first process to really understand what's going on, and later you can use the memory of the sound to play it.

Practicing different polyrhythms regularly will really free up your rhythmic language and you'll start hearing new phrasing ideas for your melodies and percussive sounds. Start with one or two polyrhythms per week and practice drumming with your hands on your knees while at work or riding the bus. You'll get addicted to it and it will make you a better musician and producer.

Tip Number 66. Making Drum Fills With Your Hands

This is a cool way to add a human element and some uniqueness to your transitions. If your production features programmed drums you can try banging out the drum fills with your hands on the tabletop – or alternatively use drum sticks – and record it with a microphone.

Convert the audio to MIDI using Melodyne or some other audio to MIDI converter. You now need to move the new MIDI clip onto your drum track and match the MIDI notes to the right drum samples.

Put the original audio file on a track lined up with the MIDI; listen to the dynamics of your organically played drum fill and adjust the velocity of your samples to get the full feel of the audio file into your MIDI.

Tip Number 67. Create Movement for Mono Synths

Having synth tracks in mono is great, because they don't take up as much space as stereo tracks and you have full control over their placement in the stereo field. However, it can sound a bit unexciting and one-dimensional at times. There are several cures for this, including the use of delay, reverb, chorus etc. Let's look at another way to create some movement across the stereo field.

First off, what is the difference between mono and stereo? Simply put, stereo means there is a difference between the left and the right channel. The bigger the difference, the more "stereo" it will sound to your brain. This also means that there is less "middle", so if you overdo it you will start losing punch and definition; anyone who has played around with a stereo widening tool knows this.

One way to create stereo movement where there is no stereo information (ie a mono track) is to fake a stereo track by duplicating the mono track and create difference between the two by altering the dynamic content, thus making the tracks move differently in the left and the right channel. Two ways to do this:

1. Duplicate the track so that you'll have two identical mono channels. Hard pan the two tracks so the first is panned 100% left and the second track is panned 100% right. Now put a compressor on the first track and leave the attack and release on a medium setting for the time being and lower the threshold until you get some compression going. On the second track, put an expander using the same attack/ release settings.

2. Duplicate the track and pan like in the above example. Put a compressor on the first track using a fast attack and a fast release. For the second track, do the opposite, use a fairly slow attack and a medium-to-slow release. The two mono tracks will be moving in different "waves" or grooves and the difference in dynamics between the left and the right channel will give the impression of movement across the stereo field.

Try experimenting with different attack/release settings to find the movement you like. Also, use the dry/wet knob on the compressors if there is one and/or try less extreme panning to control the subtlety of the effect.

Tip Number 68. The Reverse Reverb Track Technique

Reverse reverb is a pretty common technique for vocals, especially in electronic music genres. It's usually used before the first phrase to introduce the vocals in a track. It can be used for more things than that, however. It can be used as a sort of fill before a transition or just subtly placed in the background to achieve some interesting movement.

One pretty cool way to have complete control over the effect is to duplicate the track you want to send to the reverb. If the track contains several audio clips, highlight them all and consolidate so that you have one big audio clip that starts where the first clip starts on the original track, and ends where the last clip ends.

Now reverse the audio clip and insert a reverb, 100% wet, with a tail of at least a couple of seconds. Freeze the track and consolidate (if your DAW does not allow you to freeze you can record the track onto a new track, just make sure the start and the ending of the clip are exactly the same as the original clip) and reverse the clip again.

You now have a reverse reverb that runs all the way from start to finish of your dry track. You can use volume automation to throw in the effect occasionally or just keep it in there all the time to get a sort of reverse groove in the background.

Tip Number 69. Give Dynamic Movement to Any Track

Sometimes you want to get a vocal track or a synth pad to move a little more dynamically compared to the rest of the tracks. A great and easy trick you can try is sending a little bit of that track to the drum bus compressor.

This way the vocal or synth you're sending to the compressor will move along with the drums' dynamics. Keep in mind that this is parallel processing; don't send the whole signal to the compressor.

An alternative approach that may or may not suit your mixing style better is inserting a compressor on the track to which you want to give some movement, let the side-chain see the drum bus signal and adjust the dry/wet of the compressor until you hear the desired result.

Keep in mind, however, that the latter technique won't yield the exact same result as the first one since the compressor is not reacting at all to the track you are processing.

Tip Number 70. The Swinging Microphone Trick

This is a re-amping technique that might be tricky to get right and can potentially damage your microphone if you're not careful. But when you get it right it can be a very cool way to get an effect sounding like an organic Leslie speaker.

Through one of your monitors, play back the track to which you want the effect applied. Plug in one of your less fragile microphones, preferably a smaller dynamic or condenser type. Use a foam pop screen on the mic to minimize wind noise. Grab the mic cable and make sure it's of the right length for you to be able to swing it like a lasso in front of the speaker, without it touching the speaker or the walls around you.

You'll have to experiment a bit to minimize noise from the cable, etc., but it can give you a very cool and unique sound.

MUSIC
THEORY
FOR
COMPOSERS
AND
PRODUCERS

This chapter might seem a little tricky if you're not used to music theory, but if you take it slowly and do a little bit at a time it will surely be worth it in the end. It's a good idea to have a chordal instrument, like a keyboard or a guitar, on hand while reading so you can try out the concepts.

I've limited this section to the major scales to keep it concise and easier to understand. If you want to explore the minor scales (there are several), there is a lot of information to be found on the internet or in books once you've got a good grasp of these basic concepts.

Music is often said to consist of three things: rhythm, harmony and melody, although this is not always true for music of other traditions than the western tradition – an Indian raga doesn't have harmony in the sense we mostly think about it (chords). Interesting chord progressions are the inspiration for, and the starting point of, a lot of great songs. Let's get the basics under our belt so we can start digging into the creative part.

I want to make one thing clear before we begin, though; I do not suggest that you sit down and think about these principles when you're composing or coming up with a new song from scratch. Your intuition and inspiration should be more than enough at that point. However, when you're stuck for ideas or feel the need to add some excitement to your composition, using these principles to analyze what you've done so far and see what tools you can use to take it to the next level is a godsend.

Equal Temperament

Speaking of western music, we have something called equal temperament. This means that that the distance between any two semitones is the same. This is not true for the "natural scale" – a closer look at the harmonics of a given tone will reveal this. So why alter the frequencies of the notes? Well, it gives us the benefits of being able to play in all 12 keys. So even though we have to accept slightly out of tune intervals, we have the possibility to borrow chords from other keys and modulate to a different key all in one composition. This is pretty great.

If we didn't have equal temperament tuning, we wouldn't be able to play an E major chord and an F minor chord without retuning the instrument in-between. The major third of an E major chord and the minor third of an F minor chord are the exact same frequency in our tuning system, whereas they would differ by 38 cents in the natural tone series. Anyone who played with tuning in cents in their DAW knows that it's a pretty big deal to change the tuning this much.

OK, so this is pretty complicated stuff and, luckily, something we don't have to think about too much, but it is the basis of our exploration of a creative use of all the chords at our disposal.

The Melody of Harmony

Although harmony and melody are seen as two separate entities, they can actually be hard to separate from each other at times. Reharmonizing (changing the chords of) a song can really change the way the melody sounds. An extreme case in point is Antonio Carlos Jobim's One Note Samba, which uses mostly one single note as melody and lets the chords move the melody.

Being proficient at finding a variety of chords that work over a given melody and recognizing the different flavors it gives the melody is a great tool to have in songwriting, composition, arranging and even remixing.

The Major Scales

Knowing what chords you have at your disposal means that you need to know at least some of the fundamentals of music theory. I will mostly use the key of C major as an example in this article, but try to learn as many major scales as you can and also the chords that are diatonic (use only the notes in that key/scale) to the key in question.

These are the notes of the C major scale (ie all the white notes on the piano):

C D E F G A B

If you harmonized the major scale it would look like this:

C Dm Em F G Am Bdim

As you can see, the first, fourth and fifth chords are major. And the second, third and sixth chords are minor. This is true for every major key. So, what about the seventh chord? Bdim stands for B diminished and means that the fifth of the chord is lowered a semitone. The seventh chord is not very commonly used in modern music, but is found a lot more frequently in classical music.

The Function of Chords

Chords are not randomly chosen in a composition. There is a reason why a specific chord is often chosen in a certain context. Harmony is all about creating tension and releasing that tension. To understand this, and to understand which chords can replace which, you need to grasp the concept of "function". You can think about it like kitchen utensils, some tools are a more obvious choice for the job but there are other similar tools that can do it. Likewise, you wouldn't use a spatula to grate carrots, those tools simply do not share the same function. Let's look at the chords from the C major scale again and their three functions:

Tonic

C major is the first chord of the scale, it's known as the tonic. Its function is to provide stability, release and rest in the key of C. There are two more chords that have a tonic function in the key of C. These are E minor and A minor. Note that they all have notes in common, Em shares the notes E and G with the C chord; and Am contains the notes C and E.

Subdominant

The subdominant function is less stable/restful than the tonic function. It has some movement in it. Its main function is to pull away from the tonic. If the tonic equals sitting down in your favorite armchair, the subdominant is getting up and walking in a slow, comfortable pace. The main subdominant chord in C major is the F chord. Dm has the notes F and A in common with the F chord and is also subdominant. Since the subdominant chords do not create a lot of tension that has to be released by going back to a tonic chord (state of rest). they are very versatile and can usually be followed by either a tonic, subdominant or a dominant chord.

Dominant

The dominant chord is the most unstable of the bunch, it creates tension that really wants to be resolved back to the tonic. In C major the dominant chord is G and usually has an added seventh (the note F in this case) to give it a dissonant interval between the third of the chord (B) and the seventh of the chord (F). When the B resolves into a C and the F resolves into an E (the tonic and third of the C major chord), the tension is released and we get the sense of "coming home". The last chord that we haven't given a function is Bdim. It is also dominant, but as mentioned before, it is not commonly used in popular music.

In Practice

OK, let's have a look at some music. This is the first part of a verse from the Beatles tune Hey Jude, transposed to C major. Can you see how the chord progression flows in terms of the chord functions?

C	G
G7	C
F	C
G	C

Substitution by Function

One of the basic forms of chord substitution is something called "substitution by function". This simply means that you can substitute one chord for another if they both have the same function in the key you're in. If you don't understand what is meant by the term "function", go back to the previous article and review. Let's clarify the concept with a simple diatonic (uses no notes outside the key we're in) chord progression in C major as an example:

C F C G C

If we change the F chord to another subdominant chord we would have this:

C Dm C G C

Now let's do something about that tonic chord being repeated so many times. We have two more chords in this key that have a tonic function: Am and Em. How about this:

C Dm Em G Am

Pretty different from the original chord progression, but it is basically expressing the same thing. You might have to change a note or two in the melody for this type of chord substitution to work, or you can use this method to extend your original chord progression or come up with chords for a different section of the song.

Secondary Dominants

This is a concept that immediately gives you a lot of new chords to use. You now (should) know where to find the dominant chord of any key. If you're unsure, simply go up a fifth from any chord (the fifth of your tonic chord becomes the root note of the dominant chord) to find the root note of its dominant chord.

So, what if I told you that you could have five more dominant chords that can safely be used in the key you're in? We've used the dominant chord that leads to the tonic, but you can do this when going to any other chord too (I've excluded the chord formed on the seventh degree of the scale, Bdim in C major). Let's have a look at this simple chord progression in the key of C major:

C F Dm G C

Now let's add some secondary dominants. Usually the secondary dominants might last a little less time than the diatonic chords since they have the function of leading to another chord and are not really part of the key we're in. A7 is the dominant of Dm, so let's add that in front of it.

We'll also add the dominant of G, which is D7, and lastly we add G7, which is not really a secondary dominant in this scenario:

C F A7 Dm D7 G G7 C

For a more subtle approach, sometimes you can omit the 7th:

C Am Dm Em G C

is turned into:

C E Am Dm B7 Em G C

Keeping the 7th in the B sounded better to me in this progression while playing the triad version (three notes, no 7th) of E worked well. Use your ears to see what sounds the best.

A Variation on Secondary Dominants

The secondary dominants, as all dominants do, create a strong pull towards the target chord. They make the ear want to hear that specific chord. While this is a satisfying sound since it is a perfect sequence of tension and release, it can get a bit predictable at times. One simple remedy for this is to use substitution by function.

If you have an A7 that is expected to resolve to a Dm, you can use another chord with the same function as your target chord instead. Since Dm is subdominant in the key of C, we'll use another subdominant chord, namely F. Finally, you can fool the ear of the listener and let the secondary dominant resolve to a chord that is not the target chord at all. This can work well used sparingly as an unexpected effect.

Getting Back Home

The most obvious and direct way to go back to the tonic, is by going with the dominant 7th chord. In C major this would mean playing a G7 before the C. This is like getting into a taxi and shouting the destination out loud.

Sometimes this might feel too obvious and you want something a little more subtle. Dropping the 7th can make it a little bit more subtle since you won't have the dissonance of the tritone interval (more on this term below) – the 3rd and the 7th of the dominant chord that want to resolve into the root and the 3rd of the target chord. This would be more like taking a bus that goes in the general direction of your destination.

If you want to go subtler, still you can use the subdominant chords and put the dominant chord's root note at the bottom. In C major this would mean F with a G in the bass (written as F/G) and Dm with G in the bass (Dm/G).

The tritone interval is the interval between the third and the seventh of a dominant 7th chord, in other words three wholetones apart. The tritone substitution is a very common technique in jazz, it means that, instead of playing the dominant 7th chord of the chord you're heading towards, you play the chord that is a tritone up from that dominant 7th chord. Too complicated? I'll make it easy to remember: if you go up three wholetones from the root of the dominant chord, you'll end up a halftone above the tonic.

So in C major, the tritone substitution is C#7. As mentioned, this technique mostly shows up in jazz, so it might sound out of place in a composition consisting mostly of triad major and minor chords, but can be a welcome addition if you use lots of dominant 7th chords and other extensions like 9ths and 13ths.

Another route worth mentioning is the diminished 7th chord. This is a special little someone that can get you out of trouble a lot of the times when you're harmonically lost in a composition and need to get back to the tonic. The dim7 consists of four minor thirds stacked on top of each other.

There are really only three dim7 chords, because if you go up chromatically (not skipping any key on the piano), the fourth chord you hit will have the same notes as the first but in different order. Basically, a dim7 chord can resolve pretty well to any chord that has its root note a halftone above one of the notes in the dim7 chord. So the tritone substitution leading to C will be C#7 and the dim7 chord will be Bdim7.

Another way to use the dim7 chord is to put it in before the dominant chord. This is a technique commonly used in gospel music. Complete the gospel flavor by using the trick of the subdominant with a dominant root note that I showed you above:

C F F#dim7 F/G

The dim7 when used in a non-jazz context can make the harmony sound a bit more sophisticated and sometimes a bit Beatles-esque.

MODULATION

Three Ways to Change Key in a Song

You've just written a great verse and a chorus that seems to fit really well. You're happy with the melodies, but the chorus is in roughly the same melodic range as the verse. This might give the effect of the chorus not having that impact that the contrast of a higher pitched melody can bring. You can either move the melody up a third or so using more or less the same chords, but this might not sound as good as the original melody. Here's where your friend modulation (change of key) comes in.

You might have other reasons to change key in a song; adding excitement or variation in the middle eight or in the middle of the verse even. Whatever your motive, here are three ways to do it.

The Abrupt Way

This is where you just play a chord that belongs to another key without preparing the listener for it harmonically. You can prepare the listener in other ways like placement in the song, think about a song going up a semi tone in the last chorus or last part of the last chorus (this is sometimes referred to as arranger's modulation since it's not really part of the songwriting process).

This can work by surprising the listener and can be effective to give a chorus that lift. In Jo-anna says by Son of a

Plumber, the verse is in A major and ends on the dominant chord E major, which lets your ear think it will go back to A, but instead goes up a minor third to a C major. The chorus then stays in the key of C major.

Another example is the original version of Islands In The Stream; the song is in C major but jumps abruptly to a G# chord after the first chorus. This approach can work really well but will get old quickly if used frequently.

The Sneaky Way

If you want your key change to be less apparent and fly a bit under the radar, a pivot chord is the way to go. A pivot chord (also known as common chord) is a chord that exists in both the key you're in and the destination key. Let's say you're in the key of C major and you want to go to Bb (B flat) major. Let's find the pivot chords, the chords that exist in both keys. If you want an overview of the keys and their respective chords, check here (http://musictheorysite.com/major-scales/list-of-all-major-scales). In this case Dm and F are the chords common to both keys. Let's try Dm. Our chord progression could look like this:

C Am Dm Bb Eb F7 Bb

The funny thing here is that the Dm really acts as two chords; when it's played it will sound like the second chord in the C major key, but as soon as you hit that Bb major chord the D minor will be remembered as the third chord in the Bb major key. This will fool the ear and make it harder to hear when the actual key change is being done. So, if we want to come back to C major we could use the other common chord, F. Something like this:

C Am Dm Bb Eb F7 Bb F C G C

There is a variation on this technique. Instead of using a chord that is common to both keys, you can emphasize a note that is common between the two chords. For instance, you can go from a C major chord to a Ab major chord by highlighting the note C that is found in both chords. This can be done either by letting the lead melody play that note or by arranging the instruments so that note gets extra attention in the harmony.

The Apparent Way

If you want the key change to be more apparent, play the dominant chord leading to tonic of the destination key. In the example mentioned this would mean playing an F7 before going to Bb (try playing an F for a beat or two and then adding the dominant 7, this will make the transition smoother but still very apparent).

"IT SOUNDS TOO DIGITAL"
THE HUNT FOR IMPERFECTION

There was a time when there was so much imperfection involved in recording and music production. There was hiss, hiss from the console, the outboard gear, hiss from the engineer that was trying to eliminate some of the hiss from the tape machine. The synths used were all analog and there was pitch drift going on. The vocalists didn't stay perfectly on pitch and there was no way to correct every note with an algorithm. In those days engineers dreamed of linear, noise-free recording mediums.

If you've listened a lot to music from the "old days", the years before in-the-box production became sort of the norm (if we've reached that point), you're probably used to hearing a lot of subtle or not-so-subtle distortion from tubes, transistors, transformers, tape heads, etc.

Today so many perfectly pitched software instruments are used in production that the variation in pitch drift is close to eliminated. If this is good or bad in general is beside the point, but what it does affect is the way we perceive pitch.

Think of the pitch of a note as a field. The center point of that field is the exact frequency that you're aiming for, but as long as you're anywhere in that field, you're perceived as being in tune. When all the instruments are slightly off center in that field, the field widens. When the field widens, there is more "room" for the vocalist and slightly off-pitch notes will sound fine to most listeners.

Try doubling some parts with real instruments that by definition are less than perfect intonation-wise and pitch-wise. You can also slightly detune some of your software instruments.

Saturation

Sometimes the terms "saturation" and "distortion" are used interchangeably. However, saturation is really more about the means to get distortion. Back in the day when everyone was recording to tape, recording levels were a very big deal compared to the 24-bit environment we all know today. If the level was too low, you'd be too close to the noise floor, resulting in a very hissy recording. With levels too high, the tape started to saturate, meaning that the peaks of the waveform would be gently cut off, creating new harmonics in the process. This process can happen with other types of analog components such as transformers too.

There is a ton of saturation plugins on the market and some of them sound pretty great. However, saturation is arguably one of the trickiest things to get right in the digital domain, so this might be an area where you should consider going the analog route.

Great Analog Gear on the Cheap

Great-sounding analog gear might seem out of reach for most hobbyists and home studio owners. This is not necessarily true. Sure, if you're aiming for Bricasti reverbs and a rack full of Distressors and Vari Mu compressors, it will get expensive quickly.

There are, however, other ways to get your hands on analog gear that could set your mixes and production apart from the in-the-box productions that all use the same plugins.

Pedals

Many top producers and engineers swear by using guitar pedals, even when they're in a studio full of top-notch outboard gear. Guitar pedals are inexpensive and there are loads of great-sounding ones that cover effects like distortion, delay, filters, reverb, and special FX.

Guitar pedals have a lot of color; you'd be struggling to find that much character in plugins or expensive analog gear found in big studios. Don't limit your mind to thinking that they're just for guitars and the occasional synthesizer; nothing gives your drums more character quicker, and producers like Joe Chiccarelli love using guitar pedals on lead vocals, among other things.

There is the issue of impedance when you're using gear that is expecting high impedance signals like the one from an electric guitar. If you feed the input a line-level signal like the signal from your audio interface, mic preamp or synthesizer, you can get distortion and attenuation of high frequencies, among other things. This might sound cool or may be resolved if you turn down the signal you're feeding into it.

If you're aiming for a clean and hi-fi signal chain, it can be a good idea to look into buying a re-amp box that will convert your line level signal to a high impedance signal. The output from the pedal can then be routed to an instrument input on your audio interface, mixer or preamp.

Tape

Another way to go is to get a tape machine. You can get a two-track, quarter-inch tape machine for little money on eBay if you look out for them. A well-serviced Revox A77, for example, can sound lovely and can even be used for mastering. And there are few things that are more enjoyable in audio engineering than running your drum bus through a real tape machine, driving it hard and watching the reels spin while listening to the result.

Tape can do great things for your audio, it will soften transients and create very musical harmonics that will allow your bass to have weight and be heard on small speakers, among other things.

The use of reel-to-reel tape still has a certain aura among music production enthusiasts and can help set you apart from your peers and possibly attract more business.

If you don't want to go down the reel-to-reel route, you can use cassette tape as well. It won't sound the same, but a high-end cassette deck can do nice things to audio too. You can even use it as a real-time processor if you buy a cassette adapter that will let you pass audio through it.

Select Pieces

The third option is to get some of the outboard gear that is to be had secondhand for little money. If you're looking for distortion, overdriving the inputs of a preamp or mixer can give you interesting results. Classic brilliant gear like the DBX 160X compressor has been used on kick and snare drum and vocals on countless best-selling albums. And it doesn't cost much more than your average plugin compressor.

Another option is to buy a hardware reverb. Not analog perhaps, but it's still hardware and it will get you a more unique sound than using plugins (the converters will certainly give you a bit of characteristic imperfection). The

Roland SRV 2000 is an example of a reverb used extensively in the 1980s and can be had for little money.

There is a lot more of the inexpensive yet very capable gear around if you want it and look out for it.

Tip Number 71. "Four on the Floor" Kick Drum Variation

When you have the same kick drum sample playing every time and that sample is quantized to the grid of the track, it can get a bit static and lifeless-sounding after a while.

What you can do is either add a high frequency click to your sample, or you can split the kick drum into two different tracks and filter out everything except the clicky high end on one track and do the opposite on the other track.

Now put some sort of time-based effect like a phaser or a chorus on the high-frequency click. You can also choose to automate some other effect, like a reverb send or distortion, to get a bit of variation that way.

Another way to achieve this is by using a synth to play the high frequency information on top of your kick drum sample, then use the synth's modulation or play around with the filter cutoff and resonance manually.

Compress the modulated part with your original kick drum to make sure they sound like one entity.

Tip Number 72. Humanized Delays

When using programmed parts that are quantized or completely locked to the grid, you can get a bit of human life to it by using a delay that is based on a note value like an 8th note, a 16th note, etc. The trick here is to tap the delay tempo manually so that it is slightly off.

In this case the delays take the role of adding imperfections so that the dry sounds can stay locked to the grid. It may take a little bit of practice if you're not used to tapping in your delays, but when you get it right it really is an effective technique.

Tip Number 73. Manual Analog Console Emulation

Analog consoles are known, among other things, to make stereo images sound wider than they would in a DAW. One of the reasons for this effect is that there are always small differences in sound between two given channels of an analog console.

So why does this matter? Well, what exactly is a stereo sound? It is basically differences between the left and the right channel. Anything that is common to both channels will be perceived as mono and to our ears it sounds like the sound is placed between the speakers. This is called the phantom center and is basically an illusion.

If you can increase the difference between the two channels, you can make the stereo image seem wider. This is where the inherent nature of a console comes in handy: it is practically impossible to make two channels sound exactly the same due to different tolerances in the components used. There are a number of console emulation plugins on the market but most of them don't emulate the difference between channels.

The good news is that, whether or not you're using a console emulation, you can intentionally create these differences. The easiest way to do this is to insert an EQ on each track (unless you have an EQ that can do different curves for the left and the right channel you'll have to split the stereo track into two mono tracks and pan them hard left and right).

When boosting and cutting, instead of just copying the setting onto the second channel, make small changes in frequency center, Q-value and the amount of decibels you boost or cut. I really mean small, think 5–10 % difference. Since it might be weird to EQ only one side to get the right

EQ settings, it might be a good idea to use a stereo EQ on aux/bus/group and then copy the settings to the mono instances. You can make a template for this to be used on a few selected tracks. Try it out and learn to listen for those subtle differences.

Tip Number 74. Imitating Old Samplers

When people used hardware samplers such as the MPC 60 and the SP 1200, it was common practice to speed up the sound before sampling it and then slow it down again before playback. This way you could sample longer sounds than the sampler would normally allow.

When using a lo-fi type plugin that reduces bit depth and sample rate you can simulate this by pitch shifting the track up 12 semitones (you can experiment with different amounts here) and bouncing the track with the effect printed to it. Now simply pitch it down the same amount and you'll have the track back to normal speed. Since the plugin operates on different frequencies when the sound is sped up, the artifacts will be different and will bring different character than if you simply used the plugin on the original track. Sampling in the old days was done when the material was recorded to tape and mostly played back on vinyl records. Inserting a tape emulation followed by some subtle vinyl crackle can further enhance the illusion.

Tip Number 75. Tame Sharp Transients

Transients is where a lot of the excitement and groove lives. If we lose too much of them, the track will have less impact and will not jump out of the speakers. However, sharp, pointy transients can feel like torture to your ears and will probably make you turn down the volume or turn the song off completely.

Start with compression. The slower the attack, the more of the first part of the transient will slip through untouched. Turn down your speakers really low until you mostly hear the transients and start turning the attack knob one step at a time towards the fastest setting.

It's great to reference other music at a low volume like this to learn how transients are shaped in commercial-level mixes. Listening at a really low volume also minimizes the effects of unflattering room acoustics in your listening environment.

Sometimes the curves of a compressor aren't enough to tame that early part of the transient that hits your eardrum like a spike. In those cases a limiter or a transient designer might do the trick. A bit of distortion or soft clipping can also be my favorite choice at times. For this I love tape machines. Real ones can do wonders, but in absence of a reel-to-reel in your studio, try an emulation.

One of the great benefits with tape is that, while it softens the transients, it adds punch and body that can make up for the slight loss of impact you get from rounding off the transients.

DEALING
WITH PEOPLE

When I first started working in recording, it was in a studio that mostly recorded voice actors. Honestly, I was pretty clueless, I didn't really understand analog workflow (I later went to school to learn that properly) and I had no experience in working with a vocalist or voice actor.

The owner of the studio told me that every time he did a take with an actor he would compliment them heavily, whether they did a terrible job or a brilliant one. Although this approach can work sometimes, I've found better ways to deal with people; both through trial and error and through reading as much as I can about the psychological aspects of personal interaction and getting people to perform well. Let's start off with a few simple but important points.

• Acknowledge the importance of other people by always being on time.

• Clean up your language; it exudes self-control, respect and professionalism.

• Speak up confidently; don't mumble when communicating with your clients or colleagues.

• Try to cultivate an overall confident manner when working, keep your back straight and look people directly in the eye.

• Ask well-thought-out questions to let it be known that you're interested in your client and the project.

• Search for some quality about the people in the session that can be used for a sincere compliment. Deliver the compliment using that person's first name.

• When troubleshooting a technical problem in the middle of a session, appear calm and give the client the impression that you're adjusting things simply because you're striving for perfection.

Sometimes you're listening to a vocalist doing a vocal take and it just hits you like a punch in the stomach – the performance is pretty much awful. There may be a bunch of things that seem wrong to you, maybe the phrasing is off, the energy is not there and there are notes that are just too much off pitch.

Letting the vocalist know all the things that you think are wrong with the performance might just completely wreck his or her confidence and ultimately create a bad vibe that could well be hard to fix.

In a case like this I would suggest you find the key component that when fixed might subsequently take care of a few or even all of the other issues. Find a keyword to tell the vocalist; often inspiration works better than critique.

Adopt the attitude you want others to have. You've probably experienced at least one teacher who was so enthusiastic when giving the lecture that you just couldn't help but become interested. Sell ideas by being sold on them yourself.

If the client has a vague sense that something isn't perfect but can't seem to pinpoint what's wrong, find some small thing that you think can be improved and make an adjustment. Let the client know that you feel convinced that everything fell into place and that they should be very happy with the end result. The client basically wants to feel sure about the project and be happy with the result, so if you invite them to feel this way, chances are they will go along with it.

Prepare Yourself

If possible, get some rest before a session. Meditation is great for building focus. Stay away from sugar and too much caffeine or you'll be heading for a crash during the session. Right before the session or meeting, stand in front of a mirror and think about all the wonderful things that will happen and how well it all will go. Do this until you break into a big genuine smile. This will help set the tone for the whole session. Especially when you're working with people who don't know you, it's important to inject a bit of positive energy into that first encounter.

Set everything up perfectly before people arrive, whether it's having your notes well organized before a meeting with a client or having the recording chain and headphone mix tested. There's nothing worse that having to start the session by troubleshooting when you should be focusing on getting the client to be relaxed and feel confident in you.

It's important to take care of yourself so you'll have enough energy to focus on more than one thing during the session. An easy mistake to make is to focus on getting a good vibe among the people present in the room, and then miss something technical, or vice versa. It takes a lot of experience to foresee every little thing that can go wrong, so make sure you have the extra fuel to improvise and multitask.

PRACTICE!

When you're learning to play an instrument you usually practice quite a lot before attempting to play an intricate solo or join a band or an orchestra. Yet most people seem to jump head-first into mixing using a number of different tools, even though they hardly know what these really do to the signal they feed it.

Practice means thinking about every tool you use just like you would think of an instrument you're learning to play. A huge part of mixing and music production is about training your brain to perceive subtle differences, and to do this you need to be aware of what to listen for. I suggest you try at least a few of the exercises I describe in this chapter. Some might seem a bit too basic for you depending on your experience, but they really are worth doing.

Start by going through the hardware or software tools that you tend to use in your mix and spend a few hours just running audio through them and learning in detail what they do to different types of material.

Woodshedding

Jazz musicians sometimes use the term "woodshedding". It refers to isolating yourself, sitting in a woodshed practicing your instrument to get really good before you go out into the world. This mentality can be used for your mixing and production skills too. Here's a few exercises that will give you a general idea and get you started.

In your mix, solo the drums and one more instrument to which you want to apply reverb, preferably something rhythmic like keys or guitars. Now, turn up the reverb pretty loud and adjust the reverb time until the tails go silent just before the next note/chord, or the next drum beat.

When it sounds good and in time with the song, move on to pre-delay; let the attack of the note be dry and have the reverb come in right after, making it breathe in time with the music.

Unmute all the tracks and listen to the full mix; turn down the reverb until you just can't hear it. Now try bypassing the reverb, listen to the mix, and turn the reverb on again. Can you hear the difference? If you can't, turn up the reverb slightly and try again. If you can, turn down the reverb even more and see if you can train your ears to hear very subtle changes in depth and space.

Insert an EQ on a track in the mix and boost any frequency by 2–3 dB. Listen to the full mix, bypass the EQ and turn it on again. Listen to see if you can still hear the difference doing 1 dB of boost, or even less. Next, try cutting instead of boosting.

Do the whole reverb exercise again, but this time use delay instead. Try to see what using different note values like eighth-notes and sixteenth-notes does to the sound, compared to delay times that are not in time with the music.

Insert a compressor on your snare drum, slowest release and slowest attack. Adjust the attack until you hear some of the transients get compressed. The easiest way to hear this is to listen to the loss of high-end frequencies. About 6 dB of gain reduction is good for this exercise. Adjust the release until the meter has gone all the way back to zero just before the next snare hits.

Try the same thing again, but this time compress the whole drum bus, making sure the compression resets in time for each drum hit. These attack and release settings are a good starting point for other instruments in the mix that you want to pump in time with the music.

Walk around outside or sit at home and listen to cars going by, drilling, or crying babies; try to identify the frequency ranges for each sound. Can you hear the sub frequencies created when the tires are rolling against the pavement? Do you also hear the mid-range parts of that same sound? When hearing a sound through a wall, which frequencies get lost? This is a great ear-training exercise that you can do wherever you are and won't cost you much in terms of time spent since you can do it while going about your day.

Listen to commercial mixes with a low pass filter on. This is a great way to focus in on the low end and learn how it sounds in well-crafted mixes. Listen to your favorite mixes in mono. You'll find that EQ and compression choices become more apparent, and you'll hear the balance between the main elements: kick, snare, bass and vocals. This will prepare you for listening to your own mix in mono and making balance decisions.

When listening to great sounding-mixes, turn down your monitors really low and just listen to the transients of the kick and snare. Then load up your own mix and do the same while adjusting the attack of the drum compressor; you'll find that you can easily hear the difference between a 3 ms and 10 ms attack at low volume because the transients are not being distorted too much by your room acoustics.

Go Out and Find Inspiration

Analogies and metaphors are a powerful means of understanding the world around us and casting new light on old concepts. It can also work as a reminder of how much we can learn from other types of creative and artistic work; a lot of successful and highly creative people in the music industry, people like Michael Beinhorn, swear by the practice of regularly practicing or taking in other forms of art. Whether it's writing, painting or whatever you choose, different art forms feed each other.

Also, watching live acts is something that will enhance your studio chops massively. Whether it's a live rock band, a classical concert or even a DJ set, you'll get a sense of how live music sounds and what works great on a crowd. If the DJ is playing a track that works exceptionally well on the dance floor, use a phone app to find out the name of the track and go home and analyze it.

It can be very helpful to use other art forms such as painting as an analogy for music production as it may help you make some new points and stay clear of too much habitual thinking. It actually makes a lot of sense to think of a mix or a production as a painting; it can be a realistic representation of a performance or an abstract representation of an idea that's not really rooted in anything outside your imagination.

When you think about it, even a recording of a live performance is an interpretation of reality. Or an enhanced version of it, if you will. To get as far away as possible from any form of interpretation, you'd have to record a performance using only some sort of binaural recording setup, simulating the human ears. And let's face it, most of the time you're probably going to want to be more creative than that.

VOCALS

Possibly the most common, yet most unique, instrument in music across all genres is the human voice. It is a remarkably versatile instrument that can be very challenging to perform, record and mix to perfection.

Two aspects of this spectacular instrument stand out. First of all, every human being has a unique voice; even the best impersonator can't replicate the microtiming and nuances that are unique to every person (they can create a pretty convincing illusion, but analysis used for voice recognition software show that it's pretty much impossible to get it right). Second, our voices are capable of producing a wide range of sounds, from periodic (pitched, when our vocal chords vibrate in a periodic manner) to aperiodic (e.g. whispers, breaths and certain consonants) and percussive sounds.

All those types of sounds are not seldom represented in a single word or vocal phrase. So it's no wonder that it's a complicated process to capture vocals well and get them to sit perfectly in a mix.

Before diving into the deeper layers of the audio engineering and production aspects of vocals, let's have a closer look at the instrument in question. It all starts with a steady flow of air created by air pressure in our lungs. The air then moves through our windpipe, the larynx (voice box) where the vocal cords vibrate to create a pitch if we so choose. Different resonances are created when we manipulate the shape of our lips, jaw, tongue and soft palate (the soft part in the back of the roof of your mouth).

If we look at the vocal tract as a synthesizer, the vocal cords are the oscillator and our lips, jaw, tongue and soft palate form the cut-off filter and resonance knob.

Formants

The resonances that occur when we change the shape of the vocal tract are known as formants. Think of it as an EQ curve with a number of bell curves that boost different frequency-ranges. Formants are ranges of frequencies (harmonics created by the vocal cords) that are louder than the frequencies in the areas where little or no resonance is present.

Formants are what makes an "o" sound different from an "a" or any other vowel. Formants are the reason that we have difficulty distinguishing between different vowels when the pitch of a note is really high – this occurs sometimes in opera singing. When the pitch is very high, some of the formants (harmonics) fall outside of our hearing range.

Here are the average formant frequencies for three common vowels:

Vowel	Formant 1	Formant 2
i	240 Hz	2400 Hz
o	360 Hz	640 Hz
e	390 Hz	2300 Hz

Tools like Melodyne or certain formant filters let you manipulate those formant frequencies. Formant shifting can be used as an obvious effect where you lower or raise the formants a great amount to get a kind of sped-up or sloweddown feel to the lead vocals. It can also be used more subtly as mentioned in Tip 16 and Tip 51.

Reverb Choices

Trends come and go when it comes to music production in general, but the element that has possibly been most associated with musical trends is reverb. The way you use reverb can help place a song in a specific time period and it can be used consciously and effectively to enhance a particular aesthetic.

In the 1980s, reverb was abundant and the reverb type of choice was artificial digital reverb with lots of high-end frequencies surging through the air. For this sound, either go with an older outboard reverb or use an algorithmic reverb plugin and leave some of the bright frequencies in there (Tip 64 is useful here to counteract some of the side-effects of having a bright reverb).

Another reverb aesthetic that is more or less synonymous with the 1980s is the non-linear reverb. A non-linear reverb is a reverb where the tail doesn't fade out in a natural fashion like the reverb of a real space. Instead it's cut off more or less abruptly. Nowadays, most digital reverbs offer presets of some kind for non-linear-type reverbs, but originally gates were used to cut the reverb off, and this is still a valid technique. Probably the most common application for this type of reverb is to give the drums, especially the snare drum, that unnatural larger-than-life effect that can be heard clearly on *Some Like it Hot* by The Power Station.

In the 1990s everything changed. Reverb was more or less banned from recordings, and allegedly engineers could be fired when getting caught using reverb on a mix. Of course, there was some reverb used during this period as well, and the natural reverberation of the room is heard on drum recordings of this era. However, a bright, digital-sounding reverb is not something that would work well with the 90s aesthetic.

If we go all the way back to the 1970s, we encounter more of the analog side of reverb in the shape of echo chambers and plate reverbs. An echo chamber is essentially a dedicated room where a speaker is placed along with one or more microphones. A signal is sent from the console to the speaker and the microphones pick up the reverberated sound, which is sent back to a channel on the console. This way you can send the vocal channel to the chamber and have reverb on a different fader in real time. The microphones placed farther away from the speaker receive more of the "wet" sound (reverberation created by the sound waves bouncing off the hard surfaces in the chamber).

Plate were initially created to be a poor man's version of a reverb chamber, since a chamber required a whole separate room, which was a luxury not always available in the smaller studios. Plates and chambers do share a lot of the same characteristics, sound-wise. They don't sound like a real physical space in the same way a hall or room reverb does.

The reason that plates and echo chambers don't sound like a hall or room reverb is that the echo chamber has no parallel surfaces. An echo chamber will have a reverb tail that is much longer and smoother than the reverb in a normal room of the same size. We're used to being inside rooms where the floor and the ceiling are parallel, and at least a couple of the walls as well, so it's hard to make sense of the size of the room when you hear an echo chamber reverb. The same goes for plate reverbs, which are really not a room at all, but a metallic plate that resonates and creates the illusion of space. A mono plate reverb on vocals can be a gorgeous sound and instantly gives the song a bit of a 1970s vibe.

If you have the opportunity to work with a real physical plate, it's a satisfying experience for sure. There is something about the way it seamlessly blends with the dry vocals without making them sound like they're drenched in reverb that is quite astonishing. I've used many impulse responses of plate reverb, I've even made a few impulses of the plates I've used and compared the impulse response with the real thing, but sadly they don't really come that close to the real deal in my opinion.

That said, I use impulse responses of plates all the time, and they certainly have their place. But if you want to come close to the dynamic behavior of a real plate (not necessarily the exact sound), I'd go with a high-quality algorithmic reverb.

That brings us to the choice between impulse response reverb (also known as convolution reverb) and algorithmic reverb. The former operates by using a type of sample that is created by letting a sine tone sweep or a percussive sound go through a reverb. When you load that sample into a convolution reverb the actual sound that was sent to the reverb is washed away and you now have a recording of a space or a reverb unit. This type of reverb can sound very realistic and I like using them as a sort of "glue" when most tracks in a mix are sent to it to give the impression that they exist in the same space.

The problem is that impulse response reverbs are not very dynamic, they are more of a snapshot of the real thing and they're not gonna react differently if you send a bass-heavy kick drum to them or a high-frequency synth lead. This is where the algorithmic reverb comes in. While an algorithmic reverb can sound less like a real space at first glance, a high-quality one will give you a lot more detail and the option to modulate the reverb and make more interesting reverb tails.

Vocal Delays

Some of the most famous vocal delays are the slap-back echoes prominent in 1950s rock and roll. They can be heard on a lot of Elvis records, and in the 1970s John Lennon used slap-back delay on his voice more often than not.

The original slap-back echo was created by feeding the output of the playback head of the tape machine to the record head. The physical gap between the heads created a delay on the signal. The delay time could be altered by changing the tape speed on the machine (30 IPS will give a faster delay than 15 IPS, etc.). If you want to create a slap-back effect, turn down the feedback to zero (just a single echo repeat), set the delay time to somewhere between 80 and 120 milliseconds and turn up the delay quite loud so it's close to the dry sound in amplitude.

If you use even shorter delay times then you're leaving slap-back territory and moving into what can be called a "doubling delay". These can simulate, in the simplest of ways, a vocal recording of a close double of the main vocal. The delay times typically range from 30 to 50 milliseconds and can be used to make a wide-sounding vocal (use two different delay times and pan the two delays hard left/right).

If you're after a dry, in-your-face-type vocal sound, it can be tempting to leave delay and reverb out of the picture completely. However, the way our brains interpret sound will not necessarily give you what you want if you leave the vocals without any sort of ambience in the mix. Using a short delay with a single repeat and giving the instruments around the vocals a sense of larger space gives your brain that point of reference that creates that close, tight vocal sound.

Microphone Choices

Choosing a microphone for a vocal performance is often less about choosing the highest-quality microphone at your disposal and more about finding the mic that complements the vocalist's voice as well as possible.

What this means is that it should counteract the unwanted quality in a person's voice, and bring the desired qualities to the forefront. So if a vocalist's voice is very mid-rangey, nasal or bass-heavy, then you should use a microphone that is the opposite of that.

Having a dynamic microphone like a Shure SM7B, Audio Technica RE-20 or even a ribbon mic around is handy when you need to tackle aggressive vocals or voices that generally tend to sound a little harsh. Don't be surprised if they sound better than some of the higher-end condenser mics on many voices.

Trying out dozens of microphones on any given singer is not a very practical approach. Even if you're lucky enough to own that large a number of great mics, it will take up a lot of time, fatigue the vocalist and you'll probably have a hard time distinguishing between all those takes anyway.

This is where positioning the mic becomes crucial. Changing the position and angle of the microphone will change the sound in a similar more profound way than EQ – and EQ may not always be able to fix a badly positioned mic.

Where Do You Place the Mic?

I'd highly recommend experimentation when it comes to angling and positioning the microphone, but basically you get more low end by moving or angling the mic towards the chest of the singer. If sibilance is a problem, try moving the mic slightly off-axis so that it's not directly in front of the mouth but rather slightly to the side. An overly nasal vocal can be fixed by – you've guessed it – moving the mic further down, away from the nose.

Learn to hear the subtle differences that occur when you move the microphone half an inch or so. You can practice doing this on other types of sound sources as well, two good ones being a guitar amplifier or an acoustic guitar. Check out the earplug recording trick to really dive into this (Tip Number 17).

The distance between the microphone and the singer is also a very important factor. Most microphones will not sound their best if the vocalist is pressed up against the grill, and you'll increase the risk of unwanted distortion on loud notes. However, there are two scenarios where getting up close is the best approach.

The first scenario is when you're after an intimate sound where the singer is singing really softly. In this case you probably want to be able to hear all the little details and breathiness and maximize the direct-sound-to-reflected-sound ratio. The second scenario is when you're after a lot of proximity effect to give the voice some additional low end and make it sound deeper. Proximity effect is a phenomenon that exaggerates the amount of low frequencies being translated when the sound source is close to the capsule. This only occurs in microphones with a cardioid pick-up pattern.

A microphone with an omni pattern takes up sound more or less equally from all angles and does not exhibit any proximity effect, thus having a more consistent sound if the singer moves around a lot. The downside is that it will expose more of the sound of the room. So if your room doesn't have a flattering sound, you're probably better off using a cardioid pattern.

Getting back to keeping the distance from the microphone; a lot of singers aren't really aware of the fact that they're moving closer to or farther away from the mic between takes. Or even during takes. Using a pop filter can serve a dual purpose in those cases. Put the filter at the distance from the mic where you want the singer's mouth to be, adding an inch or so, then instruct the vocalist to always stay where the pop filter is barely touching the nose.

Putting a piece of tape on the floors where you want the singer's toes is another great way to get the vocalist to get back to the same position after a take or a break, especially if the singer isn't that close to the mic. It works for actors *and* singers!

Getting a Great Performance

Choosing a great mic and knowing where to place it doesn't get you very far if the singer's performance isn't up to par. Being an engineer, you're not necessarily a great vocal coach, but there are some simple things you can do that can really make the difference between a mediocre performance and an inspired one.

The first thing to consider is the cue/headphone mix. There are a number of things you can do to help shape the performance. First of all, listen to the mix and see if there are any potentially distracting elements in it. Simplifying a mix can make harmony and groove become more prominent, and sometimes backing off reverb to get a slightly dryer mix can help make it even clearer. There is a balance to consider here, however. If you go too far you might make the mix sound boring, and you absolutely want the vocalist to feel excited about the song during the recording.

Most singers like a bit of reverb in their headphone mix, and adding some compression can help the vocals sound a bit more polished, which is a good thing when you want the singer to keep the self-confidence intact throughout the session.

Although most singers are pretty specific about how they want to balance the level of their voice against the music in their headphones, adjusting the balance can be a valuable tool for the engineer. If the vocalist seems to lack power and energy in their performance, turning down their voice in the mix can really help. They will have to struggle a little to be heard clearly, and that will immediately bring more power to the performance. And, vice versa, if the vocals are overpowering you can try turning them up in the mix and suddenly the singer will get feedback that tells them they need to take the energy down a notch.

When it comes to singing on pitch, uncovering one ear so that they hear themselves naturally in the room can help a lot. For some reason, headphones can distort our sense of pitch, so it's not necessarily the case that the vocalist has a bad ear for pitch generally if he/she sings off pitch. Also, turning up the harmonic elements of the mix can help. Some singers like to use the bass as a guide for pitch, so ask about their preference.

A different approach is to ditch the headphones altoge-ther. If you're recording a band, the singer can perform in the same room if you don't mind the bleed. Or you can do the vocal take in the control room with the speakers blasting, Bono-style. The trick here is to sing facing the speakers using a dynamic mic, like a Shure SM58 or an SM7B, and to switch the polarity on the background track (this is done most easily in the DAW using a plugin to swap the phase on the master bus). The dynamic mic will minimize bleed from the monitors and the switched polarity will cancel out some of the bleed when combined with the other tracks at mix-down.

Another thing to consider is how much of recording is psychology. This seems to be doubly true when it comes to recording vocals, since it's a very personal thing and it's easy to lose confidence and feel insecure. As a producer or engineer, always be on the lookout for sincere compliments that you can throw at the singer between takes. Re-read the chapter "Dealing with People" for more tips on getting the most out of a recording session.

USING IMAGINARY

COLLABORATORS IN THE STUDIO

Collaborating with other people in a creative process can be incredibly rewarding, and there are few other ways that will help you grow quicker as an artist and a professional.

In a perfect world we'd all have constant access to great musicians, fellow audio engineers, or just friendly people with great taste and judgement. However, reality is such that many of us work alone most of the time and some of us are not that comfortable with sharing our creative process with other people.

While I do think it's a very good idea to try working with other people when the opportunity arises, here's a few ways to use the concept of collaboration without having actual human beings around.

MIDI Friends

Sometimes you're running out of inspiration or your musical ability is simply not up to par. Having some MIDI files with notes played by real players on your hard drive is a simple and effective recipe for a good-sounding instrumental part or even a new direction for your song or production.

You do have to be willing to go in and do some heavy editing when needed. Sometimes you need to change the pitch or timing, move things around and mute some parts while looping others, etc.

You can buy MIDI files from loop libraries or use ones that come with virtual instruments like Addictive Drums or EZdrummer, but my favorite way to get cool MIDI files is to go looking for great grooves in existing songs, sample a few bars from them and then convert them to MIDI.

Some DAWs like Ableton have this ability built in. Alternatively, you can use software like Melodyne or even zoom in the wave file and place the MIDI notes in the right places on a MIDI track below.

Remember to change the BPM of your session to the BPM of the sample before converting to MIDI, so that the loop starts and ends in the right places. After that you can change the BPM to any tempo you like because now you're working with MIDI. Pretty handy. Edit and tweak until it fits the music you're working on and save the file for later use.

"Audience"

Recording lead vocals on your own in the studio can be an underwhelming experience. Apart from the problem with lack of objectivity when you're assessing your own voice and performance, it's hard to find the right energy level and presence in your performance. You'll often end up being too much in your own head. This is usually a bad thing when you're performing live, and it's a good bet that it's a bad thing in the studio too, since you still need to reach an audience. There's just a time delay involved.

Imagine that you're singing in front of an audience. Closing your eyes and visualizing them is a good way to go, and make sure you make up a pretty damn fantastic audience while you're at it. This can help you project the energy forward when you're singing and lets you more easily find that extra gear that makes the difference between an OK performance and an inspired one.

Musical Performance

When Stevie Wonder recorded his early work he'd play all of the instruments himself on a number of tracks. The story told by those attending the sessions is that Stevie didn't try to sound like other musicians; he would become that person in his mind when he played, performing as kind of an actor as well as a musician.

While not everyone of us has the musical abilities of Stevie Wonder, this technique can work really well when you're looking for a certain sound and don't have anyone around who can deliver it. I've done this on a few occasions with good results. I'd say it works best if you choose a musician whose work you're very familiar with.

Take a minute to "get under the skin" of the musician you're impersonating. What kind of feel would he or she be looking for? Is it busy with lots of notes or more minimalistic? What about the tone? Are you starting to hear the rhythms or even the specific notes in your head? Try to imagine being this person, invited to your session and ready to play. Now start playing those notes.

Multiple Personality Harmonies

I don't remember where I originally heard about this slightly quirky technique, but I've used several versions of it during the years since. It's a technique for singing background harmonies on your own when the sound of a group of different singers is desired.

This is similar to the Stevie Wonder technique, but I tend not to use real artists as the archetype for the performance. To me it'd feel slightly too jokey to throw a Bob Dylan or Neil Young impersonation into the mix.

Don't overthink it, but take a few seconds to find the voice and mannerisms of the person you're imagining. Think about the body shape and personality of this fictional character. Use a cardioid pattern on your microphone and do the first take imagining this person singing it.

Create a new character for each take and move around so that you don't do all the takes from the same angle. This will help increase the difference between the voices you create by varying the frequency response of the microphone.

Evaluating a mix

It's happened to me so many times. I've been working on a mix and I feel pretty good about it, so I ask someone else to listen to it and tell me what they think. The very moment I press play with the other person in the room I start hearing things that are not working the way they should. Arrangement issues suddenly pop out at me, the high end of the vocal needs more shimmer and the automation just before the chorus isn't aggressive enough. And so on.

While it's great to have someone come in and listen to your mix, and they can surely offer some valuable perspective and feedback, that option is not always on the table.

I've found that the little shift in mindset that lets you hear things that seemed hidden to you before the other person walked into room can be approximated with some help from the imagination. The best practice I've found for this is to do this when you normally take a break.

Simply walk out of the control room and go do something else for five minutes or more. When you come back, imagine someone else is in the room to listen to the mix for the first time. If you tap deeply enough into your imagination you'll probably find that you start hearing things in the mix that you hadn't noticed before.

MANAGING STRESS –

MAINTAINING A LONG CAREER

Nowadays, a huge proportion of people who work as audio engineers or music producers are completely self-employed or at least doing a part of their work as freelancers.

Being your own boss can be wonderful in many ways, but making a living without any guaranteed income can be very stressful.

When I wrote the first edition of this book I was recovering from stress-related health problems. I had been building up my own business for about five years and I had been working from early morning, pausing to have dinner and then continuing to work late into the night. My mind was constantly going over new business ideas and worrying about not getting enough money for next month's bills.

One day my body had had enough and my legs literally gave out when I was in the kitchen cooking dinner. I was basically burned out. From that day I continued to experience severe dizziness, blurred vision, random episodes of pain in my body and exhaustion for a long time.

At the time this happened it seemed to have come like a bolt from the blue, but looking back I realize I actually saw it coming for years but kept ignoring it and didn't attempt to change my way of living at all.

Since then I've gone through professional rehabilitation, learned a lot about stress and the brain and along the way I've changed a lot of my habits. This chapter is about sharing some tools and techniques to help you last longer as an audio engineer and hopefully feel a little bit better in general.

Box Breathing

Research has shown a strong connection between how we breathe and what is going on in our nervous system. When we get stressed out the sympathetic nervous system kicks in and hormones like adrenaline and cortisol are released into our bloodstream. This tends to result in faster and more shallow breathing.

While your fast and shallow breathing may seem like purely a result of bodily stress, and not the cause of it, consciously changing your breathing pattern can affect the level of stress in your body in an effective way.

There are a huge number of breathing patterns and exercises out there. Some are backed by research and some aren't. A simple and effective technique, that got a bit of fame from the fact that the American Navy SEALs allegedly use it for stress management, is called box breathing. It's as easy to do as it is effective. You simply divide your breathing into four parts and do each of them for four seconds.

1. Breathe in (four seconds)
2. Hold your breath (four seconds)
3. Breathe out (four seconds)
4. Hold your breath (four seconds)

Repeat ten times or more. I find that visualizing the numbers as you count can help further calm your mind and switch focus from obsessive or stressful thoughts.

This breathing exercise is designed to lower your stress level while at the same time keeping you at a pretty neutral energy level. What this means it that it doesn't calm you down excessively or put you in a meditative kind of state.

If your goal is to calm to down even more when you take a break from work, or even if you want to go to sleep, you can increase the time you're breathing out. Try exhaling for eight seconds or even more than that. This might leave you a little out of breath if you're not used to it, but you'll get better at it if you stick with it. A good way to ease into it is to add an extra second to your exhalation and when you're comfortable with that you can add another second.

Single-Tasking

When we're trying to do several things at once we tend to feel like we're being really effective. And sure, at times we might get more done by doing this, but aside from the risk of making more mistakes because you're not fully focused on one task, multitasking is a really effective way to exhaust your brain. This means that even though you might get more done for a little while, you'll run out of steam more quickly and you'll have trouble staying productive throughout a whole work day.

Single-tasking is not an easy thing to do for a lot of people, especially nowadays when our phones and computers are fighting for our attention and constantly switching between different information has become more or less the norm. Depending on your level of ability to focus, there are several strategies that can serve you well.

One strategy is sitting at a completely clean desk with just your computer and a few post-it notes with your tasks written down. If you don't need to use the internet in order to complete your tasks, it's probably a good idea to turn off your internet connection. Once you've completed a task, throw that post-it note in the trash and go on to the next one. And turn your phone off or – if you're expecting an important call – keep the phone in another part of the room so you can't reach it without getting up and walking a few steps.

Another simple yet highly effective technique that will work for any type of task, not just the ones where you sit in front of a computer, is the Pomodoro technique. This technique is described in the chapter "Finish Your Productions and Get More Done". If you have a hard time leaving your phone alone I suggest you get an old-fashioned kitchen timer for this technique.

You Are What You Eat

If you want to be able to do a good job consistently and keep your stress levels in check, it's super-important not to let your energy levels go on a roller coaster ride throughout the day. Feeding your brain good fat and protein before you start your day is a good way to avoid that 10.30 dip in your mood and energy. A lot of professional mixers who work long hours (among them Dave Pensado) try to stay away from caffeine and fast carbohydrates like white bread and anything containing refined sugar.

The Heart Helps the Brain

Most of us know that physical exercise is great for increasing your stamina and fighting off heart disease and certain other illnesses. What you might not have considered are the benefits for stress management and for your brain in general. Before I became aware of the vast stress-fighting benefits of aerobic exercise (cardio), I used to rely solely on meditation and breathing exercises to calm my brain down and manage my levels of cortisol and adrenaline.

When your stress hormones are running wild it can be quite a challenge to get your body and mind to relax through meditation or simply taking a break lying down on the sofa. This might have to do with how we're wired as human beings; our stress hormones are mostly there to protect us from physical harm and are part of the fight-or-flight response. It's like our body expects us to take physical action to either fight the attacker or run away to safety before the stress response is neutralized.

Exercise is a fantastic way to lower your cortisol levels, especially aerobic exercise. If you go for a run for at least 30 minutes several times a week you can also temporarily improve creativity, according to several studies, and over time you'll get new blood vessels in the frontal lobe of the brain and the connection between the frontal cortex and the amygdala is strengthened. So, why is that last thing important? Well, the amygdala is largely responsible for triggering the fight-or-flight response and the frontal lobe can help in controlling those responses. If you want to get more information on the effect of physical exercise on the brain, I highly recommend the book *The Real Happy Pill* by psychiatrist Anders Hansen.

Just Say No

No, this isn't an anti-drugs statement, although staying off drugs is probably a pretty good idea in most cases when it comes to stress management and your mental health in general. What I'm talking about here is saying no to doing things that interfere with your work life or personal life in a negative way.

This can be saying no to doing someone a personal favor at a time when you're under a lot of stress or if the favor simply does not seem reasonable to you. The same applies to getting a task in your work place that you're not really comfortable doing and that takes time away from your actual work.

Think about it: every time you say yes to something, it establishes what you're willing to do. This might be a good thing when you say yes to the type of work you like and people come back and ask you to do more of it. Other times someone catches you in a weak moment and you agree to do something that you really don't want to do.

For those times when it's hard to say no and people try to push you into saying yes, it's great to have a tool at your disposal. Having a phrase that's polite but does not open up a discussion that can lead to you being persuaded is a pretty good idea. Saying a phrase like, "It's nice to hear that you think I'd be good at this, but unfortunately I won't be able to help you," with the second part stated with certitude, is usually effective. You can end by saying something like, "I hope it all works out," to signal that the matter is completed as far as you're concerned.

I'm not saying that you shouldn't help people out or that you should become completely selfish, but when you're under a lot of stress it can sometimes be difficult to assert yourself or think clearly about what is reasonable to accept from the people around you.

Active Rest

When we think of rest we often think of taking a nap or simply lying down on your couch doing nothing. However, this might not always be the best way to build up your energy and counteract harmful stress. Instead, try some kind of active rest. There are a number of techniques to choose from and I'd seriously encourage you to try a few and see what resonates with you. Meditation is a very effective sort of active rest. I've practiced Transcendental Meditation for many years and I find that when I actually make the time to practice it at least 20 minutes per day it makes a big difference on my stress level, mood and overall attitude. Mindfulness meditation is a good place to start. There are great apps that have guided meditations; you can start with five or even just two minutes per day and see what it does for you.

Doing breathing exercises for 10 to 20 minutes is another great way to do it. Try the modified box breathing with longer exhalation times as described above. Other forms of active rest include yoga, swimming or any type of exercise that isn't too strenuous.

Red and Green

A great way to keep track of your long-term energy reserve and keep yourself from burning out is to color-code your activities. When you write something down in your planner, simply use the color red for activities that consume energy, or you can put a red or green square around the text. Activities that consume energy include any type of work and household chores like cleaning, washing, etc. The green activities are any of the activities we call active rest, but they also include simply taking a nap or lying down for half an hour.

Another thing is that, if at all possible, you should try to do active rest before any demanding task, instead of just resting afterwards when you're completely exhausted. Chances are that you'll perform better and won't feel as burned out after you're done.

INTERVIEWS

Sound Designer and Composer Harald Boyesen

Harald Boyesen is a sound designer and composer with an impressive track record. He's been based in San Francisco, California since 2003, making music and sound design for film, commercials and live events. Among his many high-profile clients you'll find NASA, Google and YouTube, to name just a few.

How did you end up having a career in sound design and music?

In 2003 I moved to San Francisco, I was only supposed to be here for six months. Someone said, "Hey, I heard you make music. Do you wanna make music for my commercial?" I got paid 500 bucks for a Super Bowl commercial. I didn't know how much you should get paid for a commercial but I was broke and I thought that was so much money and I had no idea that you could make money off music. After I found that out it was all I wanted to do.

I have a deep love for film. Deep down inside I would like to be an art director or a director. I worked at an art school and pretty much put myself through film school by working at the school. I would get these pristine edited videos that I got to tell the emotional story to or make it feel cool or special. It was incredible and I just stuck to it. So stick to it. Just keep doing it.

Is there always a clear line between sound design and musical composition in your workflow?

There's always a definitive line between sound design and music. Especially when you're working on, let's say, a 30-second commercial and I've been hired to do both the sound design and the music. I think it's very important to keep those two extremely separate and I do passes on them almost like a computer where I'll do whooshes or camera movement highlights, whatever those sounds are, through the whole cut and then I do ambient sounds or foley in one pass. After that I'll do environments in another pass and then I turn all of that off and I do music completely separate.

The music can change to the cut of the video and when I hear it together with the sound design it gets very confusing, so I turn one of them off and end up doing passes of either music or sound design.

One thing I do to keep the sound design and music together as one piece is to keep in mind the key of the music that I'm writing so that I can tune the sound design elements to that key. This way it doesn't feel like there's this sound design element that's coming out of nowhere. I want it to feel almost like it's coming from the music. Sometimes I've even done sound design with synths that are a part of the music: instead of someone pouring a glass of water it's actually a synth with some noise and vibrato and is really part of the music track.

How much foley do you record with a microphone rather than creating the sounds with software in your computer?

Sometimes I record things but it doesn't always work. Working with directors, especially on commercials, they usually want to change things several times. They want all these options so typically I use sound libraries. I use the Sound Ideas library which we've all heard a thousand times, but typically it's mixed pretty subtly so you don't hear it too clearly. It's not like in a movie where it's very very clear.

For example, I just finished doing sound design for Hulu. They wanted a distinct sound, so I went into my favorite studio here in San Francisco, Different Fur, and I recorded different elements like glass and hits. I was creating a user experience, user interface sounds that were interacting when you clicked on things and I thought it could be cool to have different mallets hitting various pieces of material, glass being one of them. I did all this work and it sounded cool in the concept, but they didn't like it. They said there was too much texture. I was using Neumann microphones and other really nice mics and it kind of felt a little bit like a waste of time.

So sometimes I do it but I think it's a good idea to be clear with the director before you do it because you might waste your time. Especially if you're not making very much money on the project, I think it's smart to just keep it within the computer and use samples.

What type of project do you find being the most demanding?

I think the hardest thing is that every project is different and that you have to constantly create things from scratch. There is no template. The only thing that you can do is to create a production workflow for yourself that works with your own logic. I think that one of the hardest things is to really listen to things with objectivity, because you lose objectivity the more you work on something.

Also, doing things fast and being OK with the directors saying, "No, this isn't right" instead of getting frustrated. Turn your heart off and don't get too invested in it. Mix it as well as you can within a quick time frame. I think one of the hardest things with a project is that it's gonna change and you can't be too attached to it. But you wanna do a good job.

Any favorite software tools that you keep going back to?

I use Omnisphere 2 quite a lot. FabFilter Pro-L is what I use for mastering for the web. A lot of the custom pieces of music and the sound design are all going to the web, so I check my mixes on my laptop. I have to, because that's where people are gonna listen to it in the end.

I use Omnisphere pretty much all across the board, for sound design and for music. I would say I use it mostly for music and creating musical ambiences so that things aren't so dry but they also don't feel like they're in a live room. I really enjoy the textures for music composition. A lot of music composition for film needs a piano, a muted piano just always works and you'll need a background. I don't know if it's sound design or music really, but it has great textures that sit nicely behind musical compositions. And they also interact well with sound design. But I use it for both, like stingers and whooshes too.

Any favorite hardware tool?

Hands down the Sequential Prophet-6. That is the most flexible synth I've ever used in my life once I got used to it and understood the workflow. I really like the filters on it and the FX sends, it has various FX sends and it still keeps the fully analog signal path. What I also really like is that you record to audio. Sometimes with VSTs there's just so many options and with the Prophet you just record some things and you can layer and really make some interesting things that way. The Moog Minitaur is also something I use a lot.

What instrument do you use for composition most of the time?

I used to write with the guitar when I first started out. The first commercial I did in 2003, the Superbowl commercial, I wrote on the guitar with Propellerhead's Reason and then I moved over to Ableton and started writing with a piano. A keyboard is a little bit nicer laid out and I can see scales on it. Piano is the way to go.

So Ableton is the only DAW you're using now? Do you use any templates?

I only use Ableton. Specifically because I like the MIDI in it and I find the automation to be very quick. I usually take a project and I drag and drop it into new projects. I don't typically work from templates. I take pieces from projects that I feel would fit the current project.

Do you experiment with sounds in between projects?

In between projects I don't experiment. Experimentation is a really important step in the beginning of the process for a project. Experimentation and creation is the first step, then editing and finalization. Those are my three steps. In between projects I wanna do something completely different. Maybe I would experiment on my own personal music.

If we exclude formal education, what would be the best way for someone to learn sound design?

To be visual. Stay visual. Look at what's happening on screen and be able to break it down incrementally, with various elements. I think going by feel is very important with sound design, because sure you can add something, some sound, but if you don't know how to make things feel right or you're not looking at what's going on on screen, then you're just putting a sound there. So, try to do a lot of projects. Look at a lot of video and add sound to it, a *lot*.

Are there any important dos and don'ts to think about when you're working with a client?

The absolute biggest "do" is, if you're in a meeting with a client, write down and translate everything they're saying into your own words. Or take their bullet points that you get in the email and break it down into your own words and then do that incrementally. Just don't get hung up on anything, just do nothing more and nothing less than they say. That is the biggest "do" for me.

The biggest "don't" is don't get too attached. Be flexible and be OK with changes, because if you're fighting that you're already shooting yourself in the foot. Remember that as a sound designer or a composer you have so many options and you have an unlimited well of creativity inside of you. Getting too attached can disrupt further versions that might be more interesting.

Which are the main differences between producing music that people just listen to and producing music for video?

There's a listening structure for pop music or when you're making a DJ track where in pop music things should change every eight bars maybe and for DJ tracks you have a minute intro so that you can DJ it. But for video you can really switch things up a lot. Video gives you reasons for why the music is the way it is and the video is going to dictate why your music changed the way it did. I think that's the biggest difference, that you're looking at something that is telling you what's gonna change.

You're also telling an emotional story behind the story of the video. And with listening music there might be an ambiguous story but it's really a lot more rigid because there's a different pace.

Would you like to share any techniques or tricks that you tend to use a lot?

Always bus your music to a different bus than your sound design so that you can adjust the levels later on globally. And don't automate your faders, automate a gain plugin on the bus so you can make your music more dynamic, automating swells and stuff. Make sure you test it for the web too, what does it sound like on a laptop?

The most standard sounds that I use for video are whooshes and a sliding whoosh sample pack that I bought a long time ago. I send it to a long reverb with compression on the reverb and I use it to get this whooshing decay out into space. I use it all the time because clients want their camera movements to have sounds and whooshes are great for that. I have a multitrack group in Ableton from a previous project that I just drag and drop into new projects. I high pass the whooshes at 150 Hz and I use it every time.

Any specific software synths that you like for creating sound design?

Diva (U-he), Nicky Romero's Kick, Omnisphere 2. I use Ableton's Analog with lots of delay, making little pads and things like that. But Diva, Kick and Omnisphere 2 are probably my top used synths.

Do you have a favorite project that you've worked on?

I have two. NASA, I spent a week on it sitting in my studio just obsessing over it, my friend had lent me his Moog Sub 37. I applied a lot of music theory to the voice over; I would listen to just the voice over and I would shift from minor to major depending on what he was talking about. I added many many layers of various VST synths and analog synths to those MIDI chords, all doing the exact same thing. When I delivered it, the team at NASA liked it so much they said "don't change too much", which is way different from what they usually say in advertising.

Another one was the YouTube Music Awards, because it was such a different project from what I'm used to and I knew it was gonna get a lot of plays and right at the very last minute I pulled it all together so that everybody liked it. I think I did that on the last day of revision at 2 am. The directors already thought it was OK but I didn't think so. I wanted something else and I overcame something and managed to live up to my own standards, which is really hard to do.

Are you mostly hired for both music and sound design when you work on project?

Different clients typically come back for different things. Certain clients only come to me for sound design and other client will come back to me for just music composition. Newer clients will often ask me for both.

Mixing Engineer Aryan Marzban

Aryan Marzban is one of the top mixing engineers in Scandinavia, mixing for major labels and indie artists alike. He has an extensive discography that includes artists like Robyn and Tinie Tempah.

Tell me about your musical background and how you got into mixing.

Musically I started out, like most people, as a consumer. When I was a kid, MTV was on all the time and I was drawn to hip hop especially. After a while I started dreaming about becoming a hip hop artist myself and I began writing my own lyrics, but the music was sort of missing. I remember that I used to ask my dad for a bit of money and I went down to the record store where you could buy hip hop singles. In those days they often included an instrumental version of the track and I could use those for rapping. But the problem at the time was that I had a big pile of lyrics and not many instrumentals.

The change happened when a friend of mine showed me Cubase and I realized that creating the music could actually be more fun than performing as a rapper. I started producing tracks as a hobby and kept doing it throughout high school. My dad is this old-school middle eastern guy that basically gave the option of becoming something academic like a doctor or lawyer, or start working straight after high school; there was no in-between.

So I started working in the family business selling street food for about five years. It was a lot of work and finally I felt that I had to find out what I really wanted to do with my life. Somewhere I heard about the SAE institute (School of Audio Engineering) and started saving money for it. Once I started studying there I realized that there were so many other types of audio work you could do besides being a producer. My passion for the technical aspects of audio began to grow a lot at this point and led to what I'm doing now.

When did you start mixing professionally?

I started mixing professionally in 2011 so I haven't had a long career, but mainly through a lot of networking I've managed to create a body of work that usually takes a little longer than it has for me. I started out mixing for people I knew but I made sure to always act completely professional, meeting deadlines and so on. After a while, they started spreading the word that I was doing a good job and that I was reliable. To this day I try to be very accommodating;

after all, my job is to fulfill the client's vision or possibly present something better.

I always try to be flexible. If a client calls me at 2 am in a panic needing to get something done I'll tell them we'll meet up and sort it out, no problem. Being service-minded has helped me tremendously. Little by little I started getting hired to mix major label projects, but I still strive to have a personal relationship with the client, whether it's the artist or an A&R person. That's super-important to me.

How often do clients attend the mixing sessions?

Let me put it like this, I don't have just one studio where I mix. I do have my home base at Soundtrade Studios (Stockholm, Sweden) but I might just as well mix the record in the client's own studio or in a studio they choose. Some clients are fine with doing all the mix revisions via email while others want to get together and work it out in person after a few revisions.

What I usually say to the client is "OK, I've received all the files and the reference songs you've sent me; let me do a first draft and then you can decide if we can go forward communicating via email or if you want to come to the studio."

The times I tend to put my foot down is when there's maybe eight or nine emails sent about mix revisions. In those cases something isn't working in our communication so I will suggest that we sit down together in the studio and "close the song". I also want to make sure that everyone that might have something to add to the process, the producer, artist, A&R etc., attends the session, so that when I give them the final bounce, everyone has had a chance to voice their opinion.

How do you deal with mixing in a new listening environment when working in the client's studio?

I always bring reference tracks, but sure, there's a time when I feel that I don't know the sound of the room at all. I usually go back and forth between the studio monitor and my headphones until I'm familiar with listening through the monitors. What's important is that I'm there with the client who knows the studio well so I'll use him or her as a sounding board. Collaboration is so important; being a mixing engineer is not a one-man job. I always work closely with the client.

What are your favorite reference headphones?

Some people may have an opinion or two about this, but the headphones I really couldn't live without are the

Sennheiser HD 380 Pro. They are quite cheap and I know there are probably higher-quality headphones out there, but I know these so well; I know how everything translates on these, so they've become my desert island pair.

Do you use templates?

I don't have any templates like a "mix template 1". I have certain ways I like to set up a mix, I do this very quickly, importing the multitracks into a session and grouping things how I like it.

What's the most recurring musical genre you're working on?

The majority of what I've worked on is hip hop and that's probably what I'm mostly associated with. But recently it's become more like 50/50 hip hop and pop music. On the other hand, there's so much overlap these days; stuff that was called R'n'B is mostly just labeled as pop now. What I'm referring to as pop are basically songs without rap vocals.

Do you have the same approach or workflow for mixing hip hop and mixing pop?

My starting point is the same. I start by deciding what I think are the most important elements in the song. Then I compare my ideas with what the client has told me about the direction of the mix as they see it. I'm very good at getting a lot of information from the client before I start working on a mix. Since I can't be inside the client's brain I have to interpret what they're telling me and combine it with my own feeling about the song.

If there are vocal tracks, I tend to start working on those first. I do this for a couple of reasons. First of all, they tell the story of the song. Second, the vocals tend to occupy the largest number of tracks in the mix and there can be a lot of work with editing and tuning, it takes a lot of time, so I prefer to get that out of the way early on.

I look at my process like this: I set everything up the way I want it and then I go through each of the tracks and get rid of everything that shouldn't be there. You have to chop the onions before you can fry them.

Do you ever mute individual sounds or whole tracks to make the arrangement work better?

I'm not hired to mess with the production. I'm there to take what they give me and enhance it. I never add or subtract any sounds in the mix. However, I do come back to the client and suggest that they change something in the arrangement in order for the mix to work better. I let them decide. Sometimes, if the clients aren't sure they understand my suggestions, I make the changes and send that version to them so they can hear the different versions for themselves.

Is there a big difference in track count between projects and genres?

There is a bit of a difference between genres, but I'd say with most projects I get somewhere between 30 and 70 tracks to work with. In rare cases I get less than 30 tracks or as many as 130 or 140 tracks.

I do have a discussion with the clients where I tell them that if they have, for example, three snare tracks that they've blended together and they like the balance of these sounds, then they can go ahead and bounce them down to one track and just send me that. They can always send me the individual tracks later if we need to fix something. I think this is important because let's say I favor one of these snare tracks more than the others; I could change the sound of that snare completely and that may not be what they want at all.

I don't usually bounce things like background vocals to a stereo track, although sometimes I do this and mute and hide the individual tracks in the session. But most of the times I keep the tracks and route them to an aux track and work with them as a group.

What are usually the biggest challenges when you're mixing lead vocals?

Every vocal is recorded differently with different microphones and rooms, so the frequency content is something I go to right away and try to get it to where I want it to be. But the hardest part, believe it or not, is choosing the right kind of reverb for the vocals. I like reverbs that don't take up a lot of space in the mix but gives the vocal a room to exist in.

Different voices just affect the sound of the reverb differently. I have a number of reverbs that I like and I switch between them until I get close to the feel I was going for. Then I start messing with the settings and maybe insert an EQ on the aux return. I tend to go with plate reverbs for vocals, but not necessarily throughout the whole song. I might want some bigger-sounding room in a certain section of the song and then I reach for a different reverb.

Do you have a go-to signal chain when it comes to plugins on your vocal tracks?

I have my go-to plugins and I try to stick with those to limit my options a bit. I think that's a good idea in the digital realm. I have three EQs, three compressors, three limiters and three reverbs, etc. I always use these, but which one of the three I choose depends on what sounds right in each case. I try them out. If I'd try out all the plugins I have it would take me so much longer, so I created my own little "Swiss Army knife" of plugins that does the job. I know these plugins very well at this point and I know their specific strengths and weaknesses.

Are you usually able to hear the finished mix in your head before you start mixing, or is your process more of an exploration?

When I listen to the client's rough mix I can get a sense of the character of the mix and from there I can imagine how the ideal mix would sound. After that you start trying things out and all these decisions have to be made. Those decisions might lead to what you were thinking of before you started, or they might lead to something completely different.

A lot of times the artist or the producer wants to try some new ideas out because they get a new perspective of the song when they listen to the first draft of my mix. I interpret their song based on the research I've done and the information they've given me and I present my interpretation in the first draft, which is the beginning of the collaboration that leads the final mix.

How much of the mixing process is spent on writing automation?

If we're talking about all of the automation such as volume automation, filter sweeps, bypasses and so on, I'd say it's between 30% and 50% of my entire process. It's an incredibly important part of mixing, it lets you create a sense of variation even if the arrangement is really static. Automation can be either very technical or very creative, depending on what you're trying to achieve.

How do you tend to use different kinds of saturation and distortion in your mixes?

I tend to use it a lot to inject some sort of character into a track, or when something needs to be a bit more aggressive. I use plugins like Decapitator (Soundtoys) for that. Parallel distortion is something I use a lot on bass. When I do parallel distortion I duplicate the original track and use an EQ to carve out everything I don't need and then I distort it; it's usually pretty low in volume so you hear it in the background.

When it comes to vocals, it's usually rap vocals that get distortion added. It's great for in-your-face rap vocals that are supposed to be on top of the beat rather than mixed in with the music.

Do you like to edit out breaths or do you leave them in the vocal tracks?

I do some volume automation sometimes if it's a bit out of control and the breaths are almost at the same level as the vocals. But to hear a vocal performance completely without breaths is weird to me, you get the feeling that the person is holding his breath throughout the whole song. Sometimes I actually use automation to increase the level of the breath to get a more aggressive feel to the vocals.

Tell me about your process when adding reverb and delay to a mix.

I set up two or three reverbs on different auxes. They're usually plate reverbs, short ones and longer ones. I might use two different reverbs for most applications and then have a third "magical" reverb that comes in at specific moments. I use delays in a similar way. I have a really short delay that is used mainly as a doubling effect. Then I have a quarter note delay and an 8th note delay and so on. I set up a few different ones like that so I can access them easily when I mix. If I have to go through my plugin folders to find a specific delay I totally lose momentum.

Do you work completely ITB or do you use outboard gear as well?

I work almost exclusively ITB. I do run the occasional signal through the Neve console or outboard gear or bounce a track to tape, but that's usually when the client specifically requests it.

Are there any specific frequencies that you tend to give special attention?

Yes, there are few frequencies that I tend to deal with. There's usually something the annoys me at 600–700 Hz. I also listen extra carefully to the 2–4 kHz range. My favorite frequency range is probably 150 Hz and below. Bass is fun.

What are some of your favorite plugins?

One of my favorite plugins is, believe it or not, Logic's own channel EQ. It's kind of the same as with my headphones, I know that EQ so well. I don't necessarily use it for boosting frequencies though, it certainly has its limits in this regard. But I generally prefer cutting instead of boosting anyway. I also use the Digital V3 EQ from Brainworx. For Bass, I like using a Pultec clone experimenting with the boost and attenuation technique. Another tool I like using is Slate Digital's Virtual Mix Rack.

Any favorite compressors?

I use LA2As and 1176s a lot. Usually the Slate Digital ones. I also use Wave's H-comp a lot.

Are there any important dos and don'ts to think about when you're working with a client?

Number one is don't miss a deadline. Make sure that, when you agree to do a job, that you actually have the time to do it. I rather say no to an attractive offer than realize I don't have the time to do a good job. So the dos and don'ts for me are mainly about logistics.

I know you're working in the box, but is there any hardware tool you enjoy using when you're given the opportunity?

I've used Thermionic Culture's Fat Bustard a few times. It's a summing box but it's not the summing I'm after; it has a bass and a treble knob that is incredible. Not sure what it does exactly but it makes things sound so fat.

How much time do you usually spend on a mix?

The time from when I receive the files to when I send the first version of the mix to the client is usually between four and eight hours of work. I need to give myself time limit, because every time I listen to the song I'm using up a little bit of that objectivity I need. After the first draft there will often be two or three revisions. But that varies a lot too; sometimes they're 100% happy with the first draft and sometimes there will be nine revisions before everybody's happy.

How many mixes do you complete per week?

Between two and seven. When I do seven mixes in a week, it usually means that I'm working on a complete album for a client.

Slate Digital CEO Steven Slate

Steven Slate is the audio engineer who turned businessman and became one of the biggest success stories in the audio industry, creating analog-modeled plugins and hardware that rival classic studio gear available mostly to professionals working in big commercial studios.

I understand that the starting point for building your company was you recording drum hits and selling sample CDs to other engineers. What did your career in music look like at that point?

I'd just come from Boston where I had my own underground recording studio and was working at several other commercial recording studios, recording and mixing bands.

Do you remember the first piece of gear you fell in love with? When you realized there was really something about the equipment.

I was 15 or 16 years old and I got an Allen & Heath MixWizard and I remember using the equalizers on it. At the time I'd come from a Yamaha cassette four-track recorder which just had high and low shelf filters and having a four-band parametric EQ was so cool to me. And that was the first time I went "wow, this is so high-tech".

What does really good gear do to the process of mixing or producing music? Is it mostly about having a lot of different colors to work with?

The point of the gear is to help you get from point A to point B. If you wanna make a big rocking drum mix and you have a piece of gear that can help make your drums start sounding more slamming and help you get to that final point; that's the cool aspect of gear. The gear follows the vision; a lot of people mistake that, they make the vision about the gear. That's weird to me.

How did you get into plugins, did you have any coding experience?

I was making drum samples and got a team who started coding the drum samples into Kontakt. I had some success with that product, selling a lot of copies, and then (Slate Digital co-founder) Fabrice and I met and he's really the code genius, I had the ear and came up with ideas and that's the harmony that led to Slate Digital.

What's the first plugin you made?

The first was Steven Slate drums for Kontakt and after that came FG-X and Trigger.

Was there a certain point when you knew you could make a living doing what you do today?

I do. It was when I first brought my drum sample CD to the masses.

What takes up most of your time on typical day?

I'm in developing meetings with each of my different teams discussing all the products that are in development, discussing marketing of current products that we are selling and products that we are working on. It's just "product product product product product".

The way you hear sound I guess is a big part of your success; have you had a method for developing your ear or is it from experience working as a mixer?

It's experience as mixer and also experience as a plugin designer and knowing how to tweak plugins. For instance, if you're tweaking a compressor algorithm and the reference has more lows. Now, does that mean that the frequency response is different? No, it means there's a timing difference. It's the release timing that's creating a bigger low-end sound, and so on. Or if one sounds snappier, is it harmonics? Is it timing? You need to develop an ear to be able to know these things so I can tell the team that there's an issue with the release time or output saturation, or the curve, etc. It takes a lot of experience to figure out how to do that. Most of that experience came when we did the Virtual Tape Machines, because I had to learn quickly the difference between frequency response and dynamics.

Has developing plugins helped you hear sound differently when you mix?

It's probably affected me negatively. One of the things I recommend to mixers is never micro focus, always have a macro focus on a song; and I tend to micro focus more since developing plugins, which is a bad thing when mixing. But luckily I'm mixing more now for tutorials that we're doing and I think I'm getting out of the bad habits and getting my swag back.

You've emulated some really sought-after gear that not many people today have the chance to own or use. While it's really cool that so many people can now get that sound or get very close, do you feel like there is a downside to this? That some uniqueness of the gear gets lost?

Why should cool toys be reserved only for elite people with money? I think it's a terrible thing. Everyone should have the best tools available. They should be affordable and no one should be blocked from being able to use great stuff to make their art. Our job is to make music, not to sit there and wax poetic about tools.

If you started out today as an audio engineer what would be the advice you'd give yourself for having a good business mentality from day one?

The difference between my successes and my failures has really been whether I'm focused on end game or not. It's like if you're trying to get to a destination; let's say you're gonna drive across Europe. What makes more sense, jumping in the car and compressing the gas pedal? Or saying, "OK, I'm gonna go to Frankfurt and I'm gonna map out the best route checking out which routes are closed" and so on? That's really the best way to do business. You have to plan and strategize and have a very clear and focused end game. At times during my early career I didn't know how to do business and I would just get in the car and start driving, and it got me into some trouble.

Making money doing what you love, whether as an artist, audio engineer or any other type of business, means that you have to create value for other people. Passion is a great force here of course, but how about analyzing the market; how do you learn to do that when you're just starting out?

It's part talking to people studying what they're saying, and the other part is instinct, because I've done stuff people didn't really know they wanted. I had to teach them that they wanted it. The Raven and the Virtual Microphone System are examples of that. When I first brought the Raven people were saying that they didn't want it and now we can't make them fast enough.

Today whether you're an artist or an audio engineer, to succeed I think you have to think somewhat like a business owner. First, do you agree with this? And do you find that the opposite is true also, that you take inspiration from artists and how they promote themselves when you're building your brand?

Yeah, if you're building your brand whether you're a business or an artist I do think it's a similar concept and again it goes back to: what's your end game? You develop your end game and work your way backwards; what is the strategy to get to that end game?

Do you think artificial intelligence is something that will be a big part of ITB mixing and music production? Is that something you're looking into?

Well, Fabrice would object to the term "artificial intelligence", but will there be algorithms that analyze things and help make decisions? Yes. I wouldn't call something artificial intelligence if it analyzes audio, has a reference audio in its program that it uses to match. That's just using analysis algorithms. It's just about showing respect to the scientists who are actually working on artificial intelligence. It's quite a lot more complex.

Once you've reached a certain level of proficiency, as an audio engineer or as someone making tutorials

or plugins etc., apart from getting better at what you do, do you think there's a moment when you need to spend at least as much energy becoming more unique, finding your niche?

I don't think "unique" or "niche" makes any sense because [as an audio engineer] your job is to make music for an artist and if you are unique then you're not really working for the artist and their sound. You need to make it *their* unique-ness. Some people say that Chris Lord-Alge has a sound, and he kind of does, but if you listen to the way he mixes Green Day versus the way he mixed Bruce Springsteen, you can tell it's Chris because things are exciting, the drums are punchy, but they are both very unique. He's not nearly as cookie-cutter as people like to think he is. Your job is to represent the song in the best way possible. Respect the artist and the song.

Do you have a general method for achieving big goals in life, whether business or personal?

Yes. Start with the end game and go work backwards. That is a method that will always work. If you try to do it the opposite way, it will not work.

Compared to a lot of your competition, the Slate brand is very much associated with a person and I bet this

can work for you as well as against you. Was this a conscious decision early on to be the company's face and personality?

It really came out of the fact that I started off with the Steven Slate drum sample thing, so my name was already on that. So when Fabrice and I started Slate Digital it was already name recognition with the term "Slate" because I'd sold a lot of drum samples at that point. Maybe if I knew that I would be so involved 10 or 15 years later I would have thought twice about it and we would have just used some name like "Awesome Audio Digital". It's very difficult being the face of a company. It's very rewarding when things are going well but it's also very treacherous when things are not going well. It's taken me several years but I think I've gotten into my comfort zone a little bit.

Any favorite techniques or strategies that make a big difference towards a professional sounding mix?

Practice. There's no trick other than practice, work, figure things out and just keep learning. Practice. Learn. Repeat. It takes time, my first mixes were horrible and I think my mixes now are pretty good. The first time I worked with a band I was horrible at it. I'd still be kinda horrified but I know what I'm doing.

TIP NUMBER 76. DIY Vocal Exciter

Duplicate the lead vocal track and pitch shift the new copy up one octave. If your DAW or pitch-shifting plugin allows for formant compensation, this is a good time to use that function (see The Human Voice for more info on formants). You've now created an exciter track for your vocals.

Turn down the volume all the way on exciter track and turn it back up slowly until you can hear the track clearly in the mix. Now back it off slightly. When you mute this track the vocal should sound a lot duller and lack the excitement in the top end compared to when you turn the exciter track back on.

TIP NUMBER 77. "Analog" Delays

An easy way to make your digital delays sound more analog like a tape delay, like those coming off a reel-to-reel tape machine, is to use a combination of distortion and low pass filtering.

Insert a delay on an aux track and send some audio to it via the aux sends on your tracks in your DAW. Insert your favorite distortion/overdrive placed before the delay and follow the distortion effect with an EQ. With a high shelving filter or a high cut/low pass filter, attenuate the high frequencies and start driving that distortion plugin.

The trick is to find the sweet spot between the amount of distortion and the amount of high-frequency attenuation where you can get a lovely warm and crunchy delay bouncing through your mix.

TIP NUMBER 78. Sample Your Unfinished Projects

If you're anything like me, and possibly 90% of all people making music, you probably have a lot of unfinished music on your hard drive. This can be a burden for sure and make you feel guilty about all the time and energy you've spent on projects that didn't make it to the end.

One great way to remedy this nuisance without having to actually finish the projects is to make some cool and unique samples that you can use in your new projects (because you will finish those, won't you?).

You can do this in a couple of ways. You can listen to the tracks like you would listen to a vinyl record when you're hunting for samples. Another way that can give you some cool samples that you didn't necessarily hear in your head when listening to the track is to set a short loop, preferably not longer than a half a bar, and start moving the loop around on your timeline more or less randomly. You can find really cool little rhythmic samples by starting the loop somewhere between the downbeats. Try moving the loop around using an 8th note, 16th note or 32nd note grid.

TIP NUMBER 79. "Reverse Cymbal" Breath

Use the breaths from a vocal recording creatively. Copy an intense-sounding breath and paste it before a phrase or transition to add drama and intensity. This also works wonders for VO work when there's too much intensity on a single word; lower the volume slightly and add a big in-halation before it.

TIP NUMBER 80. Quick Fix for Lightness and Space

With an EQ in M/S mode on the master bus, use a shelving filter to cut some lows on the sides. It gives the mix some more space and lightness. Low frequencies are not very directional and don't contribute to stereo width, so make a habit of keeping them mono.

TIP NUMBER 81. "Noise Reverb" Atmosphere

In a convolution reverb, instead of loading an impulse response of a reverb, load up your favorite type of noise (vinyl noise works great) or atmospheric sound. Send a bit of the snare, kick, hi-hats, etc. to the "reverb" and listen to the evolving atmospheric groove, whose frequencies and rhythms follow those of the dry sounds you send to it.

TIP NUMBER 82. Automated Delay Groove

Transform a simple kick and snare pattern into an interesting groove by automating the delay time. Start with a 16th note delay on the snare and, after one beat, change it to dotted 8th notes or 4th note triplets. You can also use two different delay plugins and automate the bypass.

TIP NUMBER 83. Dragging Delays

Without changing the tempo of a track you can create the feeling that the drums or some other instruments are rushing or dragging by offsetting the delays so that they're heard slightly before or after the beat. This can be used as a subtle way to enhance a section of a song, giving it more energy or holding it back before a big chorus.

TIP NUMBER 84. The 3D Map

Try having a virtual 3D map in your mind when placing a sound in the stereo field. Move a sound towards the front or back by the use of reverb and delay. More = towards the front. Less = towards the back. Panning and Haas effect

= left/right. Lots of high frequencies = up. Emphasis on lower frequencies = down.

TIP NUMBER 85. Formant Filter Snare Reverb

As a special effect, use a vocal formant filter (an EQ curve with a number of bandpass filters) on your snare reverb. You can turn it on for an occasional snare hit and alternate between different vowels for different drum hits.

TIP NUMBER 86. Vocal Delay Automation

Create vocal contrast between different section by automating delay times. Give the vocals a quarter note or an 1/8 note delay in the verse. When the chorus hits, change it to a half note delay and turn up the feedback a little bit. This way the vocal will have more depth in the chorus. Back off the high end slightly with an EQ to create depth without obvious echoes being heard.

TIP NUMBER 87. Transient Designer EQ

High frequencies are mostly perceived in the transients. If a sound is too piercingly bright but loses presence and brilliance when you use an EQ to fix it, use a transient designer to back off the transient and let the tail of the sound be bright. Another option is to use a compressor with a fast attack and medium-to-fast release.

TIP NUMBER 88. Bass Sustain EQ

Sometimes you want to have a lot of deep lows in your mix but they can become overpowering. You might try turning the volume of the bass track down or reaching for an EQ, but then you miss some of the impact you got from those low lows.

Another way to do it is changing the length of a bass-heavy sound. For instance, if you make a kick drum shorter, the low end will have less impact and the kick drum will be heard as having less bottom end. You can shorten a kick or bass sound to clean up bass-heavy mix or increase the length to have a more powerful mix.

TIP NUMBER 89. Reverb Time Contrast

Create contrast between different sections of the track by automating the reverb time. You can use longer reverb times for the chorus to create more depth and sustain and shorten the reverb to clean up when there's a lot of things going on at the same time or where you need a tighter, more energetic sound.

TIP NUMBER 90. Gentle Low End Clean-up

If you like high pass filtering a lot of tracks in your mix to clean up the low end, try a 6 dB/octave filter. This lets you filter out a lot of low end without getting too much separation between tracks.

Another benefit of using more gentle filters is that you get fewer of the phase-smearing artifacts that steeper filters are prone to create. It's like using a gentle natural soap instead of an industrial-grade detergent.

TIP NUMBER 91. Make a Sound Come at You from a Distance

To make a sound appear like it's coming at you from far away in the distance: Automate a high shelving filter or high cut filter and gradually back it off. Automate the volume to be slowly turned up. Fine tune until it feels in sync with the filter automation. The sweet spot is when you don't hear it as a filter opening up or as the volume being turned up, but rather as a sound coming closer and closer.
Automate a reverb send or the dry/wet ratio on a reverb inserted on the track. The reverb should be gradually backed off until the volume and filter automation have reached the end, then there should be little or no reverb heard.

If you feel like getting fancy you can also automate a compressor with a low ratio (1.5 to 2) and low threshold and slowly back off the threshold or dry/wet ratio. This simulates how air compresses a sound being heard from far away and makes it appear less dynamic. If you want to get even fancier you can simulate the Doppler effect (sound waves being compressed when the sound source is moving towards you fast, resulting in a shorter sound wave = higher pitch, and vice versa). Raise the pitch by a few cents and automate it so that the pitch returns to normal by the time the movement has stopped.

TIP NUMBER 92. Get the Levels Right

Near the end of a mix, note the level of the snare (this is for your own reference, to see if you tend to mix it too loud or too quiet). Pull the fader all the way down, close your eyes, and push it up slowly until it sounds right. You can do the same thing with other key elements in the mix, such as vocals and kick drum.

TIP NUMBER 93. Whisper Track Double

You can enhance your vocals in different ways by adding a whisper track. What this means is that the singer doubles the lead vocals by whispering the lyrics. Make sure it's a tight double, timing-wise. Used subtly, it can help the lyrics cut through without changing the sound of the vocals too much. If you turn up the whisper track louder you can create an eerie feel that can be really cool when it fits the mood of the song.

TIP NUMBER 94. Give the Vocals More Weight

Duplicate the vocal track. Filter out the highs and high-mid frequencies. Distort the track and blend with the original. You've created harmonics for the low frequencies which will make those frequencies more prominent and will give more perceived weight to the sound.

TIP NUMBER 95. Correct the Effect Send Mistake

There is a surprisingly common mistake among mixers that needs to be addressed. I'm talking about inserting a processor/effect on an aux track and leaving the dry/wet knob on a value less than 100%. So why is this a problem? That little bit of dry signal that gets through can in some scenarios be slightly out of phase with the track which you're sending to the aux. Two identical signals slightly out of phase with each other will result in some frequencies being cancelled out. This can be perceived as sounding hollow, dull, etc.

In the best case scenario your DAW's delay compensation is able to keep the phase relationship intact, but then you will mess with the level of the dry sound (it gets louder as it is summed with the dry sound from the aux). The rule is that at least one effect inserted on a given aux channel should be set to 100% wet.

If you would like to receive information about free updates and new products - join our mailing list at **www.makingsound.co**